# TANTRIC MASSAGE

## Step-by -Step Guide To Learning The Art Of Tantric Massage!

Ellen Green & Mike Sanders

# Table of Contents

# Introduction

Most people have heard about Tantric massage. However, not many know the true meaning of Tantra. In today's world, where talking and learning more about sex is no longer considered to be a taboo, more and more couples are looking for new ways to keep their sex life exciting. They may be looking to improve their sex life or they may only be trying to satiate their curiosity. Tantric massage happens to be one such topic that is being increasingly opted for in order to improve their sex life, and for spicing up the intimacy quotient between couples. Tantric massage is not a new concept. In fact, it has been around for hundreds of centuries.

The origin of tantric massage can be traced back to the ancient teaching prevalent in the East. The philosophy that backs Tantra provides different guidelines for not just drawing out and increasing your pleasure. It will also help in strengthening the bond and attachment that exists between those who are practicing it. If a couple practices the techniques of Tantra, then the bond that they share will surpass the physical realm and will help them connect on a spiritual and also on an emotional level. Such a bond cannot be broken. Tantric massage is a sensual form of massage, and it will not only revitalize your body, but it will energize your mind and soul as well. It will soothe your spirit and help you to rekindle your sexual energy.

Tantric massage is all about drawing out the pleasure. In this fast paced world, where couples don't have time for anything and quickies seem to be the norm, tantric massage will help in prolonging your sexual experiences. This book will provide you with all the information you need about tantric massage.

You will learn about the basic concepts of Tantra, as well as the concept and benefits of tantric massage. There are different tips for making your experience more pleasurable. Various essential oils that can be used are introduced and also the method of making your own blend of oil. The various techniques of tantric massage are explained. You will learn ways of drawing out tantric massage and, lastly, the impact tantric massage will have on your sex life. This is a detailed guide that will explain everything that you need to know about tantric massage.

Adopting the different techniques that have been mentioned in this book will help you in rejuvenating your sex life. It will assist you in connecting with your partner and improving your shared bond. It will take some time to master the techniques, but the effort and time spent in doing so will definitely be worthwhile. You will need to be patient because tantric massage isn't something that you will be able to master overnight. Therefore, don't feel discouraged and keep trying. So, without further ado, let's get started! We wish you a positive experience.

# Chapter 1: Tantra and Tantric Massage

Tantra is a healing technique that has been around since time immemorial. This ancient technique will help in healing and soothe your body from all the minor physical, as well as the emotional bruises, that people keep enduring on a daily basis. Tantra has been and is being practiced in our society in various forms like tantric yoga, tantric meditation, tantric massage and even tantric sex. Tantric massage makes use of all the dormant sexual energy that is present in the body for attaining a superior state of sexual awareness. It is believed that this energy has got the power to unite lovers by transcending the mental and physical boundaries and help in creating a truly ecstatic experience. The resultant bond is unlike any other.

The origin of the word Tantra can be traced back to Sanskrit. In Sanskrit, "tan" means to expand, show, or even manifest. Like mentioned earlier, Tantra is a healing technique and it helps in releasing the natural energy that is present within the body. It isn't easy to master the art of Tantra, and it will take effort and time. It can take years or even several decades for performing any of the different forms of Tantra perfectly.

Having said that, it is indeed possible to learn a few basic techniques of tantric massage that will help you in magnifying the pleasure that a couple can experience.

Different individuals tend to resort to various means for relaxing and finding some peace in this busy world. Many people swear by a tantric massage for relaxing. Tantric massage is like any other regular massage. It is based on the notion that individuals who are sexually happy tend to lead a healthier life. Tantric massage involves the massaging of your entire body, including some of your sensitive areas. In this form of massage, both the persons involved should trust each other fully. Many couples have tried Tantric massage for one reason or the other, regardless of whether it was curiosity or the want of a better sex life, Tantric massage does yield positive results. Tantric massage is an intimate massage and it requires the partners to pay heed to what the other is saying. Most are under the misconception that this form of massage involves sex. However, this is nothing more than a misconception. This indeed is a sensual massage, but it doesn't involve any sexual interaction. The receiver of this massage will have to allow the giver of the massage to have complete control over his body. In most of the cases, this massage usually takes place between individuals who share an intimate relationship, but this isn't always the case. Even a trained professional can perform this massage.

Some individuals might not be comfortable with Tantric massage because it involves sensual interaction. However, if you relax, let go and trust the person performing the massage, then you will realize how wonderful it is. If you like trying new things, then tantric massage is an experience that you should definitely try at least once. To put it simply, Tantric massage will make you feel like you are on a joy ride, without having to worry about anything or any physical boundaries or consequences.

As mentioned earlier, Tantra is a Sanskrit word, and it means expansion or manifestation. One of the most speculated theories about tantric massage is that it helps in releasing the dormant energy that is present in the body. It helps in awakening the "Kundalini." Kundalini is the mythical energy that is present in the tip of the spine and when this energy is nudged from its inertia, it starts the healing process and spreads throughout the body. Tantric massage is an excellent stress buster and it helps the receiver relax and find peace. It is based on the belief that sexually happy people tend to lead a healthier life. Tantric massage will help the couples indulging in it in attaining a greater degree of intimacy and sexual pleasure as well. It can also be made use of as a medium for forging trust, love and intimacy. Tantric massage will help in bringing the couple closer.

Tantric massage is an erotic massage and it requires the mind and spirit of an individual to be free. This is achieved by awakening the dormant sexual energy that is present in the body. A regular massage will help in soothing minor physical and mental bruises. The main difference between a regular massage and a tantric massage is that in tantric massage, every part of the body is massaged and it isn't restricted to only a particular area. It can also be thought of as a medium that is capable of traversing the sexual energy that is present within your body. The different strokes and touches used in tantric massage are comparatively light and fluttery when compared to the strokes that are used in any other type of massage such as deep tissue massage. Even though tantric massage is an erotic massage, the main aim of this massage isn't penetration. You can think of orgasms as a bonus. It will bring you and your partner closer on various levels. It isn't just a physical form of letting go of stress. It is all about love, respect and intimacy shared between the partners. There's an obvious impact of tantric massage on an individual's sex life. The reason for this is quite simple. Tantric massage helps in freeing up all the dormant sexual energy that is present in the body. When this dormant sexual energy is unleashed, a person's sex drive will experience a positive change. The best way in which you can get your partner engaged in this would be by openly discussing the idea of tantric massage with him/her. Don't hold back on any details or any apprehensions that you and your partner might share. Share your doubts or even any reservations that you or your partner may have about tantric massage in advance. So, take a deep breath, relax and let go. This is the only way in which you can enjoy this activity.

Tantric massage will make you feel like you are in a state of trance where there are no physical boundaries. The concept of time and space ceases to exist and no problems will seem to be important or you probably will forget about your worries. Here's a general overview of how a tantric massage would have to be performed. The receiver will have to recline on their back with pillows propped under their head and a pillow covered with a towel placed under their hips. Their legs should be placed slightly apart, and knees should be slightly bent. Aromatic oil would be made use of for gently massaging the person's abdomen, chest, thighs, toes, feet, nipples and their fingers as well. Make sure that the oil used is slightly warm. Every single part of the body should be massaged. This will trigger your senses and awaken the dormant energy that's present within the body. According to the ideas of Tantra, the whole body needs to be massaged, and this includes the 'sensitive areas' as well. These delicate and intimate areas are not only the centers of sensuality and lust but also the source of joy and fulfillment. Tantric massage will make you feel relaxed and yet truly aware of yourself. Information regarding the different techniques that can be used for performing tantric massage has been explained in the coming chapters.

# Chapter 2: Essentials of Tantric Massage

Tantric massage is a traditional massage that is based on the principles of Tantra. This is a varied style of meditation, and it is a ritual that is performed for freeing the mind and body from all the unwanted accumulated stress. Not only does it help in relaxing the body, mind, and soul, but it has got various health benefits as well. Regular sessions of tantric massage can help in curing various issues like muscle pain, migraines, impotency, and much more. This particular form of massage will help in increasing the sex drive and also help a person in regaining their lost vigor. Tantric massage has got set rules and requisites that should be followed for a better experience. There are certain essentials that one should know about before performing a tantric massage and they are mentioned below.

## Opting for an intimate space

To derive the maximum benefits from a tantric massage, it is really important to select a private space. The general atmosphere should be playful and relaxing. Unnecessary objects that would distract one's attention should be removed. All the gadgets like phone, laptop, tablet, etc. should be put on silent or should be switched off. The place that you have chosen should be quiet and intimate. Select a bed that is comfortable, the pillows and the bed linen needs to be soft. The room shouldn't have any harsh lighting.

## Creating a relaxing ambiance

You will need to create a magical ambiance. The ambiance or the surrounding should be conducive towards making the person feel relaxed. The room should be such that it stimulates all the five senses. Make use of flowers or aromatic candles. You can also make use of incense sticks as well. Don't opt for anything that has got an overpowering smell, keep it light and pleasing. Fresh flowers will brighten up the room as well. Light a few candles instead of opting for tube light or opt for anything that gives off a soft light. You can make use of various perfumes and some soft music for creating an appropriate environment.

## Lie face down

The person who is receiving the massage will have to lie face down, at least initially. It is widely accepted by Tantra experts that most of the important pressure points are located in the back of the human body. This doesn't necessarily imply that the entire massage needs to be carried out in this manner. Depending upon the stage and the type of the massage the receiver gets to lie on their back as well.

## Constant breathing

In Tantra, breathing practices are extremely important, and the same applies to tantric massage as well. Continuous and stable breathing not only increases the flow of oxygen in the body, but it also helps in relaxing the mind and muscles of the person as well. According to the strokes of the massage, if the receiver can control his breathing, then he will truly get to relax. Taking in slow, deep, and long breaths will help in relaxing your body and make it more enjoyable.

## Controlling the strokes

The strokes while massaging shouldn't be rushed; it should be done slowly and deliberately. One should be careful about the kind of strokes used, and care should be taken to not hurt your partner. The enjoyment factor of tantric massage depends on the slow and gentle movements. Every part of the body needs to be given special attention. Long, smooth, and circular strokes should be made use of while massaging a person for arousing their senses. Tantric massage is about experiencing the body to the fullest, and this can be achieved via loving and gentle strokes.

## Mutual intimacy

It is extremely important that there should be mutual intimacy between the massage giver and the receiver. Positive energy is generated during a session of tantric massage, and this should be utilized by those practicing it. The receiver should feel the warmth of the massage giver throughout the massage. Establishing a good rapport is important. The objective of the massage is to awaken the senses with a series of touches and strokes. Well, if of the people involved in the massage feels either awkward or uncomfortable then it would defeat the purpose of the massage. You will need to set a few ground rules for making the experience pleasurable for both the parties involved in it. For instance, the loving and gentle caresses wouldn't go well if you talk in a professional, curt, and clipped tone. The sharp contours of language would defeat the sensual nature of the massage.

## Essential oils

Make use of aromatic essential oils during the massage instead of regular oils. Essential oils are great, and they give off an aroma that can be quite soothing. You can make use of more than one essential oil. Making use of a balanced combination of essential oils does have a better effect than making use of a single one. More information about different essential oils has been provided in the coming chapters.

## Relax your partner

At the beginning of the massage, you should try and relax your partner by massaging the meridian line of their body. Tension, restlessness, and even stress can prevent a person from opening his senses and massaging this bundle of nerves will make their body pliant and help them enjoy the massage fully. It is ideal to start the massage by massaging the areas that are affected due to stress. Beginning by massaging the back, shoulders, and neck is a good idea. This will make the receiver relaxed.

# Chapter 3: Benefits of Tantric Massage

The busy and hectic life that we lead these days affects both men and women, and it causes several physical, emotional, and even sexual disorders. Stress doesn't discriminate, and it could trouble a person belonging to any age group, sex, or age. People need some relief if they want to enjoy their life to the fullest and they also have to replenish their strength to keep up with their hectic lifestyle. Massage can help in providing the much-needed comfort and help you relax.

Among all the different types of massages that exist, tantric massage is gaining popularity. The main aim of a tantric massage is to provide you with a sensual experience that will also help in improving your health. Even though it is erotic, it helps the whole body to relax and has got several benefits. The different benefits of a tantric massage are mentioned in this chapter.

### Stress Buster

Stress has become an impossibly pesky part of our everyday

life, and it is quite difficult to the pressure of having to make constant decisions and of working long hours, juggling between work and family, all these cause immense stress. However, tantric massage can help you clear your mind, make your body feel light, and help you relax. You can let go of all the tension and stress. Therefore, a session of tantric massage is recommended whenever you feel stressed. Stress is something that is capable of making you feel miserable, and if it isn't handled properly, it can cause several health problems as well.

### Sex education

In many cultures around the world, sex education isn't adequate, and this leaves both the genders unprepared for any sexual interaction or even sensuality. A tantric massage is the best way in which you can learn about your body. It provides you with a serial interaction that will help you to understand how your body works. It provides you with an insight into how your body works and the different parts that will make you feel different sensations. When you do interact with your partner, it will be helpful to know beforehand itself what excites and pleases you both.

### Premature ejaculation

Premature ejaculation usually tends to occur due to the pressure of performance. In most of the societies and cultures, men are considered to be the "doers, " and this does put an added pressure of performance of them and causes them to ejaculate prematurely. Tantric massage helps in taking this pressure off them and lets them just enjoy the sexual act. When there isn't an expectation of them to perform well and without any specific goal in mind, men can perform well sexually. This will help in rectifying the problem of premature ejaculation. Tantric massage will help in teaching you to enjoy the moment, and during intercourse, it would also improve a man's ability to hold off his climax for a while longer. It is all about drawing out the pleasure to make the experience more intense.

## Orgasm in older men

As the time passes by, and while the body starts aging, the hormone levels in the body tend to decline and because of this older man feel little or even no sexual arousal and this means that they aren't capable of reaching an orgasm. Tantric massage can be beneficial for older men. This sensual massage helps in stimulating their senses and also helps in the production of the sex hormones and thereby helping them deal with problems like erectile dysfunction and the lack of achieving an orgasm.

## Women and sex

In most of the cases, women don't enjoy intercourse. This could be caused due to various reasons ranging from their lover's inability to please them or even their lack of knowledge about their body. Women are sensual creatures, and it takes them a while longer to achieve an orgasm. Most might not even be aware of their bodies or what they like and dislike. Tantric massage will help them in understanding their bodies and their needs better. It will help them in deriving greater pleasure and even sensuality during any form of sexual activity.

Tantric massage helps in awakening your senses. It is sensual, we tend to perceive the world around us through our senses, and the awakening of the senses sharpens this perception of ours. Tantric massage is a therapeutic massage that has various health benefits. It can help in relieving body pains and aches, stimulating your immune system, and increasing your fertility as well. Many women can't orgasm, and tantric massage helps in integrating your mind and body thereby facilitating their ability to reach an orgasm. Tantric massage tends to be empowering on various levels regardless of the characteristics of an individual. Tantric massage also helps in providing the greatest form of relaxation and pleasure for your mind, body, and soul without having to reciprocate.

Tantric massage involves the massaging of all the parts of the body. Having one's genitals massaged is quite a fulfilling experience. It also helps in creating a conscious connection between all the areas of a person's life. A massage without any expectations is quite a liberating experience. Tantric massage helps in letting go of the illusion of separation that exists and remedies this divide that exists in every individual's life. It can also pave the way for a full-body orgasm.

For a person who is shy or who has gone through a lot of suffering, tantric massage might be more therapeutic than a regular massage. When their receptiveness and confidence starts to grow, they might be open for a complete tantric experience. Tantric massage is all about celebrating an individual, their strengths and remedying their weaknesses. Since it is a full body massage, it requires the individuals to let go of their fears as well as inhibitions for a pleasurable experience. Tantra is all about celebrating and cherishing one's body. There is nothing sinful about it. Tantra followers believes that the body is a temple within which the soul lives.

Tantric massage has got various benefits to offer. The benefits slightly vary from men to women. Women experience sex and sexual energy in a way that is different from men. Men are usually considered to be sexual creatures, and women are usually sensual creatures. Tantric massage has got the power to change the way an individual would approach sex. It is quite an amazing experience.

Tantric massage will help men learn to enjoy and understand the manner in which they can experience sexual pleurae throughout their whole body instead of simply focusing on the lingam. There's more to sexuality than just their penis. The different movements with sexual energy that is quite phenomenal. Also, this pattern can help men to experience a full-body orgasm or go through a multi-orgasmic state. Yes, you read it right. Multiple orgasms aren't a myth. Like men, women will also be able to attain multiple orgasms provided they let go of control and let go of themselves. There are no expectations; there are no rules. It is all about enjoying one's sexuality without any restrictions. Pleasure isn't restricted to the female or male genitalia. and the techniques used in tantric massage will help men to create a connection between their penis and the rest of their body. In this manner, their whole body would be vibrating

Like women, even men tend to store their traumas and other negative emotions and experiences around their genitals. This could be due to any traumatic event or occurrence like childhood abuse. Most of the time this remains unknown, or any critical self-image may be caused due to excessive self-judgment due to any emotional stress. Regardless of the reason of origin of these negative feelings, they do exist. Tantric massage will help in getting rid of these blocks and will help men get confident about their sexuality. The loving and the safe environment, coupled with a caring partner, make this massage exceptional.

Men will also learn about receiving pleasure without having to touch or give anything back in return. During a tantric massage, men simply need to take a step back and relax, while their partner does the massage. On a psychological level, most men are not used to giving up control, and they are more likely to be expected to be "performing." They tend to receive most of their pleasure by touching, grabbing, looking and even giving. They only need to let go and relax for enjoying this kind of massage. Well, relinquishing their control and placing their trust wholly in their partner can be quite a turn-on for the partner as well. In giving, they indeed are receiving as well. Relinquishing control can be quite erotic. Being aware that you are the reason for all the pleasure that your partner is experiencing is quite a rush, and it holds true for both men and women.

In continuation of the above point, men do understand women better after a tantric massage. By relinquishing control and being submissive, they will be able to understand what it feels like to be receptive and this will make them more sensitive. Let someone else lead them for a change. Women, this is your chance to take control. The same applies to women as well. If the receiver is a woman, then her partner gets to have unrestricted and unbridled access to his partner's body. Perhaps, being vulnerable wouldn't have ever felt this good.

Men will also be able to experience high levels of pleasure without this pleasure being coupled with an ejaculation. This will make them excellent lovers. This particular massage technique will help them in harnessing their sexual energy. To put it simply, it will allow them to hold off for longer. They will be able to engage in sex for a longer time without the need to ejaculate, and they control their sexual energy that will help them do so. For women, an orgasm is simply a bonus of a tantric massage. Their bodies are designed in such a manner that they can keep going even while experiencing an orgasm.

Men and women will also benefit from tantric massage because it allows them to deepen their spiritual bond with their partner as well. They will get to understand the manner in which they should use their sexual energy and then channel it towards higher levels of their being, something that goes beyond sex. They will learn to open their hearts and love fully, bare their souls to their partners and it will obviously let them get more creative about with their sexual acts as well. It will help men form a bond with their partner that surpasses any physical bond that they might previously have had. A bond that goes beyond physicality is quite strong, and it will deepen the relationship.

Bottom line: To sum it up, tantric massage is not just a sensual massage that helps in providing sensual pleasure. It also has many other health benefits. Tantric massage can improve your sex life as well, regardless of your gender. Both men and women can derive great pleasure from it.

# Chapter 4: Essential Oils

Do you crave love, intimacy, romance, sexuality, some sensuality, passion, better libido, cuddling with your partner and more? Well, the answer would be an obvious yes. Everyone pines for and deserves to have a sex life that is passionate, exciting and sensuous as well. In this chapter, let us take a look at the different essential oils that act like aphrodisiacs that you can make use of during a session of tantric massage. Essential oils can definitely help you in enhancing the massage. The scent, along with touch plays a great role in improving the intimacy quotient between partners. During a tantric massage, all the senses should be stimulated for creating a better experience. A sensual mood can also be set up by making the ambiance more sensuous.

When it comes to sensuality, essential oils have got a lot to contribute. There are cooling and warming oils. The cooling oils will help in calming down the nerves, and the warming oils will help in increasing and exciting your libido thereby turning up the heat in your sex life. These oils will help in opening things up and getting started. Let us discover the secrets of the essential oils that can be made use of during the tantric massage.

There are various oils mentioned in this chapter. Not all of the oils might seem best suited for you, but having a general idea of which oil should be used according to a particular situation will definitely come in handy. As they say, the devil is in the details. Getting the small things right will help in setting the tone of the massage and create a better environment. Some oils are believed to incite a sexual feeling and then there are some that can help in making it more sensual. So, why don't we get ourselves acquainted with the essential oils that act as aphrodisiacs?

**Rose**

It is probably difficult to find an oil that's more romantic than rose. This is also referred to as the essential oil of love. It does help in opening your heart to receive all the love and strength from your loved one. It will also help a person in loving himself and get rid of any negative feelings they may have about themselves. All the feelings of unworthiness and fear can be shooed away. Rose helps in stirring desire, enhancing positive feelings of confidence and self-esteem, lifting your spirits and getting rid of grief. It improves the circulation of blood, helps in dealing with problems of erectile dysfunction, semen production, uterine functions are improved and it alleviates stress. It also offers a lot of hormonal benefits like reducing the intensity of PMS and supports menstruation, helps in dealing with cramps and also menopause.

## Ylang-Ylang

It helps in slowing down a racing heart, calming your nerves and relaxes your mind and body. It works well on emotions and acts as an aphrodisiac especially during times of bereavement. Regardless of the situation, ylang-ylang helps in providing the much-needed balance for an evening out of your hyper-emotional state or makes you feel better when you are upset. It has got a calming effect and is helpful, especially for making your sexual experiences deeper and more intense. It helps in evening out your rapid heartbeat and also shallow breathing. It soothes away the negative feelings of anxiety, fear and worry and instead gets you in a mood that's receptive of some loving!

## Sandalwood

Sandalwood is one of the oldest perfumes that has been known to man. It's been in use for at least 400 years. It is an excellent oil for relieving tension and also for relaxing your muscles. Sandalwood can also be made use of for calming your blood pressure. In India, sandalwood is one of the most used ingredients and is combined with rose for making aytar. This smell is sufficient to relieve pressure and stress. Add some sandalwood essential oil while a tantric massage is taking place to help your partner relax further.

## Rosewood

Like sandalwood, even rosewood has got a calming effect on the mind and helps in instilling feelings of both confidence and improving your self-esteem. It helps in cutting through depression and produces a more positive outlook towards life in general. It instills feelings of hope and optimism. These positive emotions will make the experience more sensual. Only when a person is open to receiving their partner's love will the massage become more sensual.

### Cardamom

This is a common domestic spice, especially in India and regions of the Middle East. Cardamom has also been a part of traditional Chinese and Indian medicine for more than 3000 years. Cardamom has got a spicy smell that can help in calming the nervous system and relieving the mental fatigue that seems to be plaguing everyone these days. Cardamom is a really good reliever of strain on the nervous system.

### Clary sage

This has got some excellent benefits. It has a relaxing effect, facilitates in generating emotions of euphoria, feelings of well-being and is a really good aphrodisiac. If you are looking to introducing some creativity to your love making, then make use of this. It helps in putting things into perspective and helps in creating thoughts that are positive and inspirational as well. It also has the effect of balancing your hormones. Clary sage will definitely help you in spicing things up.

### Cedarwood

Cedarwood has a nice warming effect. The overall effect is

very gentle on both the mind and body. It smells wonderful and is an excellent option for a massage. It helps in getting rid of stress as well as muscular tension in the body. Why don't you give this amazing scent a try in your tantric massage session?

### Neroli

Neroli is popularly referred to as orange blossom and this scent can uplift the mind and also calm all your senses. It is a natural aphrodisiac and is commonly used as well. It helps in making the individual feel more confident and get rid of negative feelings like anger. It soothes your heart and calms you down. If you feel like your partner has got a lot on his or her mind, then make use of this for calming their frayed nerves.

### Patchouli

Patchouli can uplift one's mood. It is not only a great stress buster but also helps in elevating anxiety and tensions as well. It promotes an overall sense of well-being and calms down your nervous system. Nervous tension does no good and this helps in letting go of it. A person will be more receiving if their nerves are calmed and this will make the experience more sensual.

### Jasmine

Jasmine has a pleasant smell and it has aphrodisiac quality as well. It works on both a physical as well as a mental level.

This makes you emotionally balanced and cures your frayed nerves and elevates depression. Stress and exhaustion are the worst enemies for your sensuality. Jasmine essential oil can help you in getting rid of these emotions and, instead, fill you with an active fervor.

### Lavender

Lavender is an all around healing oil and is commonly used for making a person feel at peace and relaxed. This fragrance can soothe your body and set the mood for some passion. Introduce lavender oil into your tantric massage by mixing two drops of it for ½ teaspoon of any carrier oil and gently rub it over your lover's heart.

### Geranium

This is fragrant oil that will balance your emotions and also gets the blood flowing. The balancing hormones will start getting circulated throughout your body and make the person using it more relaxed. Five drops of this in the massage oil will dispel all the negativity you may feel.

### *Cinnamon*

Cinnamon would definitely remind you of warmth. Add this oil for adding some spice to your relationship. A few drops of this can clear your mind and stimulate you sexually. This is great for improving your skin and nervous system as well.

Starting out the massage with relaxing oil will definitely help in shaking off the feelings of your mundane life and relieve all the stress that burden you at any given time. It will fill your partner with positive feelings that can be transferred to your bedroom as well. The world that we live in fails to give importance to the need of relaxation. Most of us willingly strive and even put unnecessary strain on ourselves and run ourselves dry. The stressful lifestyle can be quite a buzz kill. One of the ways in which you can improve the shared intimacy between you and your partner would be by getting them to relax. Learning to relax and taking it slowly can improve the passion between couples. People tend to carry their insecurities into the bedroom as well. The following are the essential oils that you can make use of during the tantric massage depending upon your requirement.

Essential oils that act as aphrodisiacs are jasmine, patchouli, rosewood, rose, sandalwood, neroli, clary sage, ylang-ylang, vetiver and amyris. The oils that can help in relieving anxiety are Roman chamomile, geranium, juniper, cypress, clary sage, frankincense, neroli, rose, ylang-ylang and mandarin. The oils that can help in relieving nervous exhaustion are tea tree oil, ylang-ylang, thyme, geranium, grapefruit, lavender, rose, rosemary, cardamom, clove, mandarin and basil. Make use of vetiver, ylang-ylang, mandarin, chamomile, and bergamot for dealing with restlessness. Jasmine, rose, rosewood, clary sage, ylang-ylang and jasmine can be made use of for battling sexual insecurity. Add a few drops of these oils to your massaging oil to create a better experience. For a full body massage, it is recommended that you make use of a blend of oil that consists of about 50 drops of your preferred essential oil and about 4 ounces of carrier oil like coconut oil, argan oil, sesame oil, sweet almond or even jojoba.

Essential oils are usually mixed with different carrier oils for making aromatherapy oils. These oils are then made use of during aromatherapy massage. Each of these essential oils has got a different therapeutic benefit and an aromatherapy massage helps in channeling these therapeutic properties for refreshing an individual. More information about aromatherapy massage has been provided in the coming chapters. In the next chapter, you will find all the information that you will need for making your massage oil.

# Chapter 5: All About Massage Oil

Most of the people starting out with massage think that grabbing a bottle of hand cream or even body lotion would be perfectly fine for a massage, or worse - they think a dry massage would be fine. If you want the tantric massage to be sensual and relaxing and you want to spoil your partner, then you will need proper massage oil, something that will be absorbed into their skin and soften it while allowing for smooth and steady movements of the massaging strokes. If tantric massage were considered to be a form of art, then the medium used would be the massage oil. Learning to make your massage oil will not only be easier on your pocket, but it will also help you in orchestrating the massage according to your desire and leaving your signature behind. Once you have decided on the foundation and have experimented with your personal style and preferences, you will be able to surprise your partner with a massage that they will remember forever.

## History

Oils and aromatherapy aren't new and have been around for a long time. Take a look at the Bible, for instance. Mary Magdalene anointed Jesus' feet. Not only was she making use of essential oils, but she was also doing so through massage. Mary was aware of the power of the massage. It's a way to relax, relieve stress and to show interest in your partner as well. Oils have been around since longer than Biblical time itself. Around 2700 years before the birth of Christ, the Chinese were already making use of different herbs and burning oils. The Egyptians are known for making use of oils during the process of mummification, and they also made use of the same herbs and oils in their daily life as well. For instance, Cleopatra had made use of the exotic smelling jasmine oils for distracting Marc Antony during all their business meetings per se. The practitioners of Ayurveda in India have been known to have made use of aromatherapy as well as massage as forms of medical treatment. In ancient Greece, oils were made use of in aromatherapy, medicine and for making cosmetics as well. Romans made use of oils after bathing and Aztecs had learned to cultivate various herbs and plants. In the Far East, around 980 AD, the art of distilling had been developed and this lead to the modern process of making perfumes. Nearly every civilization had made use of nature's bounty and made use of various oils and massages.

A massage that makes use of essential oils is quite a luxurious sensation and it is quite magical. The slow and languid strokes coupled with wonderful scents create an unforgettable experience. When your partner takes the time out for not only selecting the oils, mixing them and creating a particular massage oil, and then applies the same to your whole body, it is his or her way of telling you that you absolutely deserve to be pampered and that he or she thinks you are truly beautiful and loved. On a psychological level, essential oils, as well as massage, do much more for the soul than just the physical benefits that they offer. The primary focus of this chapter is on providing you with all the information that you will need about essential oils that are used for a massage. You will need to keep in mind that all the oils that have been mentioned are made use of because of their medicinal properties. Some essential oils shouldn't be used on a mucous membrane and aren't fit for internal use. Some oils might be okay for some but might be too intense for someone else. Once you start experimenting with the essential oils, you will need to remember that a little goes a long way. A few drops of essential oil, when combined with the massage oil, are more than enough. While you are creating a unique blend, your signature scent should speak through. Don't mix too many essential oils. Stick to about two and not more than three essential oils in a particular massage oil blend.

## Base Oils

For the base oil, you should always opt for light oil that has a pleasant scent. Almond oil is a safe option. Do not make use of any nut-based oil for a person who is allergic to nuts. Ask and don't presume. The last thing that you would want during a sensual tantric massage is for your partner to go into anaphylactic shock. That would be disastrous. Here's a list of some of the base oils that you can use.

**Sweet Almond**: You needn't mix this with any other base oil; this means that you can use it 100%. This is light oil in both texture and color and has got the different benefits like helping with itching, dryness, relieving soreness and inflammation as well. Caution: not to be used for a person with nut allergies.

**Avocado**: This oil should be combined with oil like a sweet almond in the ratio 1:9. It is heavy oil and might leave the skin feeling really heavy and greasy.

**Avocado Pear**: This oil is excellent for those with dry skin and should be mixed with different base oil in the ration of 1:10. That is avocado pear oil should be used at only 10%.

**Borage seed:** This is another 10% oil, and it should be mixed. This is ideal for dealing with premature aging of the skin, stimulation and the regeneration of skin cells and skin conditions like multiple sclerosis and eczema.

**Cocoa butter**: This oil needs to be warmed up because it is solidified at room temperature. This is a perfect medium for dry skin.

**Coconut oil**: You needn't mix this with any other oil and it can be used for all skin types. Coconut oil is soothing oil and is very easily available. It needs to be warmed up and has a wonderfully nutty smell to it.

**Corn oil**: Another oil that can be used for all skin types. It is easily available and is soothing to use.

**Hazelnut**: You needn't dilute this oil before making use of it and it can be used for all skin types. It has also got the properties of an astringent.

**Jojoba**: this base oil should be diluted down to 10%. It helps with different skin conditions like psoriasis, acne and even inflamed skin. It can be used for all skin types and is good for hair as well.

**Peanut oil:** This is suitable for all kinds of skin and doesn't need to be diluted before using. It can be made use of for all types of skin ailments and conditions. It does have a strong aroma and can be heavy on the skin as well. Allergy to peanuts is common, so be careful while using it.

**Safflower oil:** This can be utilized at 100% and is suitable for all skin types.

**Sesame oil**: It needs to be diluted and should be used at only 10%. It suits all skin types and is effective in treating psoriasis, eczema and even arthritis. It does have a strong scent, so do smell it before making use of it.

**Soybean**: This is another oil that can be used at 100% and you don't have to dilute it. It suits all skin types.

**Sunflower oil**: Once again, perfectly suitable for all skin types and doesn't need to be diluted before using.

**Wheat germ**: It should be used at only 10% and is good for all types of skin. It helps in treating eczema, premature aging of the skin and eczema as well.

## Mix and Match

Once you have decided the base oil that you want to use, you should transfer the same into a dark glass bottle and store it in a dark and dry place, away from sunlight. Avoid storing the oil in plastic bottles. While selecting the essential oils that you would like to work with, you should keep in mind the way the scents would work together. Add a few drops of the essential oil to the base oil and see how it works. Cover the container tightly and then gently shake it so that the oils have blended well. Then all that you need to do is rest it for a few hours. After a few hours, go back and check, see how it smells once it has blended and matured. You can adjust the proportions according to your liking.

Massage oil is best used when it has been slightly heated. You don't want the oil to be extremely hot, but just a little above the body temperature. Instead of pouring the oil, take some in a shallow bowl and dip your fingers in it for spreading. Be generous with the amount of oil that you are using. Essential oils tend to have their properties, and you should keep these properties in mind while making use of them. There are some that are relaxing, others that can heat up the mucous membrane, while others are refreshing and relaxing. If you suffer from high blood pressure, then it is best to avoid hyssop, rosemary, sage and thyme oils. Licorice might also elevate blood pressure levels. Angelica oil should be avoided for people with diabetes. If you happen to enjoy tanning beds or even tanning outdoors, then it is best to avoid essential oils like grapefruit, orange, lemon, lime, ginger or any other citruses. It can make the skin hypersensitive. Consult the doctor regarding the usage of any essential oil during pregnancy. It is all about blending the essential oils well. You can mix chamomile and sandalwood for creating relaxing oil and combine cinnamon, rosemary, lavender oil with a base of sweet almond for creating a mix that not only smells wonderful but also provides a dash of heat.

Men tend to enjoy oils that have a woody or a spicy smell, whereas women tend to opt for floral scents. Try and blend these two fragrances for creating your signature scent. Experiment and see what you like the best. Take into consideration the properties of different essential oils that have been mentioned in the previous chapter.

It is easy to make your own massage oil provided that you know the different combinations that work together. Select the base oil and select your favorite therapeutic essential oil and mix them together. You can make use of these massage oils while giving any massage. You will learn more about aromatherapy massage in the coming chapters.

# Chapter 6: Tantric Massage Techniques

Like mentioned earlier, massage is a great way in which tension can be relieved and it does help in improving the circulation of blood and energy throughout the body and also helps in sexually arousing your lover. Massaging is mutually satisfying, and it helps couples in exhibiting their intimacy for each other. This age that we live in everyone is starved for touch, and a massage is the simplest and quickest fix to this problem. You might be wondering if it is easy. Well, you don't have to be a certified masseuse for being able to give a good tantric massage. The most important aspect of a good massage is the desire of wanting to please your lover. Here are a few suggestions.

Setting the mood and creating a romantic ambiance is the best way for getting started. Dim the lights, burn some fragrant candles or mild incense, play the music that your lover enjoys and that relaxes them and, lastly, make sure that the room is comfortable and warm. Well, you both will be creating some heat on your own in a while, but till then it is important to keep the room at a temperature that is comfortable because you both will be naked. You can make use of perfumed mineral oil; massage oil or a combination of the above. Make sure that you are using some oil, or else it wouldn't be a pleasurable experience.

## Start with the back

Two tablespoons of oil would be more than enough to get you started. Pour this oil into your hands and then rub them together so that the oil is slightly warm and nice to touch. Then you will need to place your hands on your lover's back. Start from the lower back and move upward until you reach their neck, around the shoulder blades and then back down, over the butt and the rosebud.

## Hand slide

Now that your lover's back is well oiled, you will have to place your hands such that they are parallel to each other and then slide them down on either side of the spine, massaging downwards from the neck to the buttocks. Then move your hands all the way over to the neck, then the shoulders and down your lover's arms till you reach their fingertips. Keep repeating this motion for at least six times. While you are doing this, don't forget to ask your lover for their feedback. You can do what they like and if your partner isn't the talkative sort, then maybe you should make sure to keep the strokes gentle and slow. Remember, it is all about giving as much pleasure as you can to your lover.

## Pull-ups

This move will add a slight variation to the massage. As you are moving your hands along their body and stroking your lover's sides, then try alternation one hand and then the other. You should start out by placing your hands on your partner's hips and then gently move your palms towards their spine. Keep moving your hands towards their waist and pull them up towards their spine. Then you should take your hands towards the side of the chest and pull it up towards the spine. Place your hands under their armpits and pull your hands upwards towards the spine. Make sure that you do this on both the sides and not just one.

## Kneading

If you have had any experience kneading dough for pizza or even for baking, then this technique will be easy for you. If you haven't, then start out by gently squeezing your lover's back and then buttocks between your thumb and the fingers. Then repeat the same motion with the other hand as well. Now you should slide your hands to a different area on the back and repeat the same process. Keep doing this until you have covered all the parts from their neck to their buttocks. The pressure that you apply will depend on the flesh that's there. For instance, chubby areas like buttocks can take more pressure than the neck where there is less flesh. So go on and squeeze a little bit harder. You can also spread the butt cheeks and knead further. This technique can be stimulating for the receiver.

## Feather stroke

Before you have moved towards the thighs, focus on the lover's neck and caress it. Keep on caressing the neck, arms, shoulders, back and their buttocks as well with just your fingertips. Use the least amount of pressure, and it should feel like they are being stroked with a feather, do this for a couple of minutes. If you have fingernails, then you can lightly run your nails along their body and gently scratch them. Be careful not to hurt your lover during this process. You can move your fingertips in circular motions, long fluid strokes, or even side-to-side caresses. The light and tickly caresses and strokes will simply build the sexual anticipation because your lover won't be able to anticipate your next move.

## Foot caress

You will probably need a little more oil so don't forget to take some oil into your palms, before spreading it on your lover's body. Make use of the hand slide technique on the calf and the thigh slowly. Follow the hand slide with the kneading technique and then move onto the feathery caresses. Do this for one leg at a time, and you will have to repeat the same order of techniques on the other leg as well. Feet are erogenous zones, and they do deserve some attention. Take one foot at a time and then smother it in oil, spread it around the ankle, then the heel and even between the toes. Make use of your palm and slide it over the bottom of your lover's foot. Do this a few times and gently rotate each toe in clockwise and then in counter clockwise motion. Gently tug on each toe and slightly pull it away from the body. Depending upon the reaction of your lover, you can vary the pressure that you are applying.

## Turn your lover over

By the time you turn your lover over, you will notice a smile playing on his or her face because this massage is relaxing and deeply sensual as well. Continue the massage by shifting your focus to their stomach and then the chest or breasts. You will learn more about the breast massage in the coming chapters. You will need to rub some oil in your hands and then place them on the center of the stomach, move them towards the nipples and back down again. Repeat this a few times, and it helps in moving the energy along their body. Female breasts are sensitive, so be gentle with them. The male chest is capable of handling more pressure, and a firmer stroke can be used.

These are the general erotic massage techniques that can be made use of during a tantric massage and you will learn more about it in the coming chapters.

# Chapter 7: Massage Guide

In this chapter, you will learn all that you need to know about giving and receiving a tantric massage. The different ways in which you can help you partner has been discussed in detail. A typical arrangement would be for one partner to receive the massage and then return the favor, but you get to decide how you want to go about this.

For a tantric massage, it is best advised that your partner is lying on a mattress or a comfortable flat surface or table. After you have prepped the space to be both pleasing and sensual, the next thing left to do is start off with sensual touches and a general relaxing massage before concentrating on your partner's erogenous zones. The idea behind this is quite simple; it is about bringing your partner to a highly aroused state and then letting them stay in that state for a while.

For men, this can be done through either verbal or nonverbal communication that would allow their level of arousal to be slowed down, changed or even stopped before their climax becomes inevitable. For women, this can be done by massaging their G-Spot or even with clitoral stimulation coupled with a breast massage. This can bring her to experience multiple orgasms. The main aim of the massage is to stimulate and arouse your partner sexually. Remember, an orgasm is just a bonus for them. You will learn about stimulating your partner and also the basics of how you can go about the tantric massage.

## Preliminaries

You will need to take some time out and create an environment that is appealing as well as sensual. The importance of having the right ambiance cannot be stressed enough. It is critical to show to your partner that you care about them and want to pleasure them. You can start out by just turning off the phones, and you can also place a Do Not Disturb sign on the door. Illuminate the room with soft lighting given off by candles and or small lamps, burn some fragrant candles or even experiment a little until you find something that you both like. The massage giver should make sure some incense is lit so that the aroma fills the air. Turn up the heat because you will both be naked and it shouldn't be uncomfortable. Keep the gloves, lubricants and oils within reach and then cover the massage table or surface with a blanket and then drape a sheet over the table that can be made use of for covering your partner. You can make use of additional pieces like faux fur of feathers for making it more sensual. Play some relaxing music. Some people might be comfortable with a pillow or rolled towel when it's placed under their knees, head and ankles. Women might be more comfortable with a pillow placed under their hips. If this is the first time you are trying out tantric massage with your partner, and then feel free to check that their fingernails are clipped neatly, and it wouldn't hurt their partner. There's one similarity between both men and women and it's that they both require some form of lubricant when their genitals are being massaged. The use of a lubricant will make the experience more pleasurable, and it will also prevent irritation of the skin. There's one difference, though. You can make use of oil based and even water based lubricants on men, but you should only make use of water-based lubricants for women. Instead of searching for any specific lubricants, you can simply make use of the massage oils that you have read about in the previous chapters. Either you can make your own massage oils, or you can even purchase them. Depending upon your choice of fragrance, you can select a particular one. You should always keep the massage oil nearby. Always take some oil in your hands before applying it on your partner's body. Take some oil ad gently rub it between your palms to slightly warm it up.

Throughout the duration of the massage, including the relaxation phase and the genital massage phase, it is crucial that the receiver feels comfortable while making comments and requests regarding the massage. The receiver is supposed to be able to express to the giver anything that might be getting in the way of his or her pleasure. Requests for the touch to be harder or lighter, asking for a break and so on can be incorporated only when the person is comfortable with communicating the same with the giver. These comments and requests are also signs that the receiver is finally paying attention to his or her emotions, feelings and pleasure. Some people believe that sex or any sexual act can bring up a lot of buried emotions or issues. When someone starts crying or seems to be in an emotionally distressed state, then make sure that you are there for him/her. Ask them what they need instead of simply assuming what they might need. It goes without saying that both the receiver and the giver need to be fine with going ahead with tantric massage. Both the partners need to be aware that this relaxation massage can lead to sexual encounters due to its erotic nature. It is best that the partners communicate about their expectations from the massage to avoid any embarrassing encounters. A situation could come up where one partner is trying to shift the massage towards a more erotic side while the other is enjoying the relaxation massage without the need to include any sexual activity. Therefore, to avoid such uncomfortable situations it would be better to discuss this topic beforehand. It is better to go into the massage without any unnecessary expectations.

## Giving the massage

The first thing that you have got to do is relax your partner's body. There may be certain specific ways in which you and your partner are used to connecting. If you don't know how to go about it, you can establish a connection with your partner by gazing into his or her eyes, by sharing loving endearments, gentle caressing or even by synchronizing your breathing. When you both feel that you are ready, then you will need to get your partner to lie down on the managing table or the chosen surface. Start out by focusing your concentration and resting your hands on your lover's upper and then lower back. Then perform a soothing massage on their back, move towards their legs and even feet. The basic principles of this are that your hands should be in constant contact with your partner's body and you should move your hands in a steady rhythmic movement. While giving a massage make sure that you are using good techniques and are making use of body mechanics like making use of your body weight for giving deeper strokes and gliding smoothly, don't lean too much over the managing table and keep your knees slightly bent for supporting your weight. Once you have got your partner to relax, then you can have him or her turn over so that they are facing you. Start out by massaging their chest, arms, abdomen, hands and neck and so on. Every part of their body needs to be massaged. When you are moving towards giving your partner a genital massage, it is important to make sure that you are gazing into his/her eyes, as if seeking permission to go ahead. If your partner has any apprehensions, then make sure that you have discussed and addressed those apprehensions. The aim of a tantric massage is for a person to let go and enjoy the pleasure that their body is capable of giving them. With practice, you will be able to use the levels of arousal and excitement of your partner and can change or modify your massaging strokes accordingly. Tantric massage can be an amazing experience and it will help in developing an intimate bond with your partner that goes beyond the physical realm.

## Pleasuring the male sex centers

One of the basic principles of a male genital massage is that you will need to change, slow down or stop what you are doing before he reaches the point of no return. The receiver has got to signal his impeding orgasm. Verbal cues and gestures can be made use of for signaling the same. This process of repeated peaking can at times help men have multiple orgasms without actually ejaculating. Repeated peaking helps in delaying the orgasm and when it does come that orgasm would be like no other. The main objective of this massage is to provide maximum pleasure. Ejaculation does provide pleasure, but it usually leaves men feeling tired and fatigued. If you and your partner have decided to massage each other alternatively, then it would be advisable to massage the woman first. Encouraging your partner with some dirty talk is exciting. However, make sure that there isn't too much of talk involved. Alternatively, make it a point that only the massage giver gets to talk. Letting your partner know either through verbal or nonverbal cues that you are excited by their pleasure is quite a turn on. It isn't necessary that the man needs to have an erection throughout the duration of the massage. In fact, some massage strokes feel better when the penis is soft. Therefore, men, you needn't worry about whether or not your penis is erect. Just lie down and enjoy the excellent massage.

## Genital massage strokes:

Different massage strokes can be made use of that would provide immense pleasure. Unless your partner has expressly mentioned it, it is a safe bet to assume that firm and consistent stroking would feel good for him. In this section, you will learn more about the different strokes that you can make use of during the tantric genital massage.

### *Healing stroke*

This is when the man's penis is resting on his belly. The giver has got to cup his testicles in one hand. The heel of the palm of her other hand should glide up and down the underside of his penis, from the base to the tip of the penis.

### *Anvil stroke*

With one hand, the giver has got to stroke the penis from the tip to the base. When the giver's hand reaches the bottom, she's got to release the grip on the penis. In the meantime, her other hand should continue to repeat the same stroke from the top of the penis. This will help in creating a repetitive and alternating motion that would be quite erotic.

### *Climbing the mountain*

The giver has got to take the receiver's penis in one hand, and gently and sensuously caress the base of his penis for about ten seconds and then give a quick up and down stroke once. She has got to repeat this sensuous stroke a few times and keep caressing. After caressing for a while, she can gradually increase the strokes. Caress for ten seconds and give two quick up and down strokes, then later on caress for a few seconds and give three quick up and down strokes and so on. Keep on doing this until the receiver can ejaculate.

The giver and the receiver get to decide how they would like to end the massage. If you choose that you want to finish the massage with him ejaculating, then keep on massaging till he ejaculates and continue to do so even after his orgasm or until your lover ask you to stop. Once you are done with the massage, simply lie next to your partner and enjoy his contentment along with him.

## Pleasuring the female sex centers

Female response to sexual acts is different from the sexual response of men. It is distinct in the following ways. Female sexual arousal is closely linked to the emotional state, and the feelings of warmth and compassion expressed towards her partner. Women can achieve their climax in two different ways. One is through the stimulation of the G-Spot, and another is through the stimulation of the clitoris. Women tend to think of the G-Spot orgasms as deeper and the clitoral orgasms as distinctly sharper. The preference of sexual stimulation varies considerably from one woman to another. Female arousal does take longer to build, but it does last longer and is usually more intense when compared to the climax that men usually experience. Women are also capable of having multiple orgasms if the stimulation continues through and after the first orgasm. The previous point mentioned is the reason why there's a difference between the tantric massage techniques used for men and women. Since women are capable of enjoying multiple orgasms, it does help to keep the massage going on through one peak and then to another.

## Types of stimulation

The preferences of women regarding clitoral and G-Spot stimulation are quite varied, so being attentive and listening to her input would help. Usually, women prefer having their entire vulva stimulated by rubbing it gently, followed up with clitoral stimulation and finally having their G-Spot stimulated. Neither clitoral nor vaginal stimulation tends to feel good unless the woman happens to be in a high state of arousal. During a genital massage, the giver might have one hand free, which he can make use of for teasing her and gliding it all over her body. Play with her nipples, massage her perineum or simply caress her body while you continue to pleasure her. More information about the genital massage has been provided in the coming chapters, but for now, here are a few ideas that you can work on.

### *Clitoral*

When massaging a woman's clitoris, it is important to understand what she likes the best. Start out by gently massaging the clit in circles around and make sure that your finger is well lubricated while doing so. Proceed to do so until you get instructions that are more specific or till you find something that she enjoys. Vary your technique slowly and make sure that you have established a rhythm for your movements. Some women tend to feel clitoral orgasms are better when their vagina is being stimulated simultaneously. This can be done by inserting a finger(s) into her vagina and massaging the vaginal canal while gently rubbing her clitoris. Before inserting your finger into her vagina, make sure that she is well lubricated and aroused. Clitoral stimulation is an important part of tantric massage.

### *G-Spot*

The G-Spot is the area that's present near the front wall of a woman's vagina; it is right behind the pubic area, about two inches inside the vagina. When you feel a slight ridge inside the vagina, you have found the G-Spot. Pressing and massaging the G-Spot can be extremely pleasurable. This can also lead to female ejaculation if the G-Spot has been properly stimulated. Female ejaculation isn't urine. It is just liquid expelled through the urethra. One easy way for stimulating the G-Spot is by inserting a well-lubricated finger into the vagina and rubbing it by gently curling your fingers upwards. The pads of your fingers would be rubbing against her G-Spot. The second approach is to rotate your fingers inside her vaginal passage to apply even pressure against all the areas.

### *Verbal and non-verbal encouragement*

It is quite helpful to include some verbal as well as non-verbal encouragement while massaging your partner. A few hot words can make all the difference. Tell the receiver something sexy about their body. Perhaps you can tell the receiver that you enjoy seeing them in a vulnerable position that you like the way their body reacts to yours. Whispering simple endearments into her ear during the massage would make the experience more erotic for your partner. Most women face sexual difficulties that stem from an internal worry that perhaps her partner is getting tired of pleasuring them, or the pressure of having an orgasm. This does make it quite a stressful experience for women, so a few simple things that would let your receiving partner know that you are enjoying the pleasure that she's experiencing can be quite a turn-on for her.

You and your partner can decide the manner in which you would want to end the massage. It doesn't always have to lead to intercourse. Instead, the two of you can simply cuddle and rest for a while. This is up to you.

# Chapter 8: Tantric Massage-Methods

## Different methods

The goal of the tantric massage is to let you transcend the physical boundaries and attain a state of total consciousness of your body, mind and soul. This is a state of awareness and pure bliss. Therefore, the methods that are made use of would alternate between massage and movement, filled in with peaceful and compatible silences. These particular extremes will be of help for both the massage giver and the receiver enjoy this experience fully. The result of this massage would be that you would feel refreshed and rejuvenated, not just sexually, but physically and emotionally as well. Tantra will help the couple in connecting with each other on a higher level, and the same is obtained in such a manner that it increased the intimacy they share and is easy once you get the hang of it. Teachings of Tantra concentrate on the philosophy of living in the moment. It will let you experience the feelings of being fully in control and also help in relinquishing the same. Let go of any thoughts regarding immediate release and satisfaction, instead, focus your energy towards delaying your gratification. Follow the three rituals mentioned in this chapter, and the results will pleasantly surprise you. Don't forget that the main aim of the tantric massage, it isn't about an orgasm. Like mentioned earlier, an orgasm is simply a bonus that is more than welcome, but this shouldn't be the driving force.

One of the critical concepts upon which the tantric massage depends is chakra. The entire philosophy of Tantra rests on the existence of chakras within the human body. Chakras can be thought of the vortices of energy in the body. There are seven major chakras and several other minor chakras. The major chakras are aligned along the spinal cord. It is believed that when all the seven chakras are aligned in the body, it brings enlightenment to the individual. Chakras help in harnessing the energy that is present in the Cosmos and also help in connecting with Divinity. These seven chakras affect the sexuality of a person. Therefore, let's take a look at the manner in which they affect our sexuality.

The first chakra is the Root Chakra, and it is considered to be the basis of the human energy system. It governs an individual's need for safety and security. This chakra is located at the base of the spinal column, and it is important to have a well-balanced root chakra for forming all sexual connections. This chakra helps an individual to trust their partner. Unless you are feeling safe and secure, you will find it difficult to connect with your partner. For sharing your energies in an open manner, it is essential to trust your partner. The root chakra is responsible for letting you trust your partner.

The second Chakra is the Sacral Chakra, and it is present between the root chakra and the belly button. This chakra governs the sex organs in the body. Feelings of guilt and shame can negatively influence the sacral chakra and would prohibit an individual from enjoying sexual intimacy like the one they are supposed to. Acceptance is the aspect affected by this chakra. Unless and until you accept yourself as a sexual being and your partner as well, you wouldn't be able to enjoy intimacy.

The third Chakra is the Solar Plexus Chakra, and this is related to appreciation. This chakra is present above the belly button and right below the sternum. It is associated with power and vitality. When this chakra is balanced, it lets an individual to indulge in a sexual act in a selfless and generous manner. Letting go of expectations is an important aspect of Tantra, and this chakra is responsible for it.

The fourth chakra is the Heart Chakra, and it is the center of love in the body. It governs an individual's ability of not just loving but being receptive to love as well. It is located near the heart. Any blockage in the energy generated by this chakra is due to the fear of loving yourself and also of loving others. Once this chakra is well balanced, a person would be able to indulge in passionate and profound sex.

The fifth chakra is the Throat Chakra is related to self-esteem, creativity, and positive expression. It is located in the area around the throat. Sex is a form of self-expression, and when this chakra is not clear, sexual expression will take a back seat, and this will, in turn, affect your sex life. Only when you are feeling positive about yourself will you be able to let go of all your fears and enjoy a sexual act and be intimate with your partner.

The sixth chakra is the Third Eye Chakra is located in the middle of your eyebrows, just above the eyes. This chakra governs your sense of intuition and wisdom. You will be able to enjoy any sexual act only when you let go of yourself and trust your intuition. Only then will you be able to connect with your partner beyond the boundaries of the physical realm. A person will struggle with intimacy if there isn't any harmony between the partners.

The seventh and the final chakra is the Crown Chakra. This chakra is responsible for your spiritual connection, and it is the seat for divinity. When this chakra is open and well balanced, you can let go of everything around you and live in the moment with your partner. The energy from this chakra helps you in forming a spiritual bond with your partner. When this chakra is blocked, it is difficult to find orgasmic release.

When all your chakras are well aligned with those of your partner, you will be able to connect with your partner on a physical, emotional, and spiritual level. Tantric massage is also about forming a bond with your partner that goes beyond the physical nature. Therefore, it can be said that tantric massage helps in balancing your chakras and waking up the dormant chakras in your body. Here are a few tantric massage techniques that you can incorporate.

## Positive pole massage

The positive poles in the body also work in the manner that is similar to the poles of a battery. The poles in the body are responsible for sending and receiving sexual energy. Positive poles massage concentrates on these poles that are present in the body and these poles make a person feel sexy and alive when they are positively charged. The steps to be followed for giving this massage are mentioned as follows:

The man has got to lie down on his back, and the woman starts rubbing his pelvic region and this includes his genitals. There is no need or hurry to push him towards his climax. Keep him on edge, while promising a sweet release after a while.

The second step is to massage his third chakra; the Solar Plexus Chakra that's present above his belly button and along the lower end of his ribcage while keeping the energy that is generated within his body. To facilitate a smooth movement while massaging him, make sure that your hands are well oiled.

The third step is to massage his fifth chakra, his neck and shoulders as well. The fifth chakra is the Throat Chakra and while massaging it makes sure that you are making use of your fingertips on the sensitive skin around the throat and the neck.

For making your partner feel all the dormant sexual energy that is present in his body to start moving, you will have to place one hand of yours on his forehead and the other one on his genitals.

Now, switch places with the woman so that she is lying face down on the massaging surface. In this manner, both the partners get an opportunity for experiencing the bliss of getting a tantric massage. Start out by massaging her second chakra, the sacral chakra, while massaging this chakra make sure that you have included several gentle strokes in a circular motion in a clockwise direction.

Then move onto massaging her chest and this includes massaging her breasts as well. Make sure that you are massaging the area above her heart. This will help in improving the circulation of blood in her body.

The third step of this massage is to place a finger right on the bridge of her nose and then start stroking upwards and towards her hairline very gently. This will massage her sixth chakra and open it up.

## Fusion massage

Fusion means two things are merging together as one. One of the main principles of tantric teachings is that our bodies are made up of bioelectrical systems and we are designed in such a manner that our energy is capable of getting merged with the energy of another person. This is the basic rule of the fusion massage, and it has been explained as follows.

Sit on a comfortable surface while facing your partner so that your palms are touching his and gently hold onto his wrists. The next step is to pace the middle finger of your right hand on your partner's heart and your partner has got to do the same. This is the area where the Heart Chakra is located. Take turns to caress each other in a gentle and slow manner. The partner who is receiving the caress is supposed to sit still, and this helps in building some anticipation. Now, you have got to shift into a yab-yum position. In this position, the male partner has got to sit cross-legged on the floor and the woman has to straddle his lap and wrap her legs around his torso. Don't let the caressing stop and stay in this position for a while. After a little while, you can shift into the star position. In the star position, both the partners have got to lie on their backs in such a manner that the hands of one partner can touch the other partner's feet. The advantage of this position is that it gives both the partners a chance to calm down and blow off some steam. When you can touch and stimulate each other's chakras, it opens them up and helps in forming a psychic connection between both the partners and helps them connect on an emotional level.

## Chakra massage

You might be thinking that all this talk about chakras seems complicated. However, it is really easy to understand the way chakras work. These chakras can be thought of as the doorways to the Cosmos, and it is crucial that your chakras align with the chakras of your partner. When your chakras align perfectly with those of your partner, it will mean that you are both perfectly compatible on a physical as well as a spiritual level. This particular massage will help in relaxing you, and it will also heighten your senses thereby magnifying your ability to seek and enjoy pleasure. Like mentioned earlier, this will also assist in bringing you and your partner closer to each other. This massage is all about massaging all the six chakras that are present in the body.

The first thing that you are supposed to do is make sure that you and your partner are breathing in sync with one another. By making use of two of your fingers, start gently massaging the pubic hairline of your partner for a few minutes and then let the palms of your hands rest at that spot for two minutes. The second chakra that is situated near the region of the lower belly should be given similar treatment as the first chakra. Make sure that you have made use of sufficient oil so that your fingers can gently glide all over your partner's body. Start massaging the third chakra in the same manner. The third chakra is located at the solar plexus, the region below the ribcage and above the stomach. Keep repeating these steps till you have covered all the chakras that are present in the body. Making use of the circular motion while massaging the chakras will help in opening them. While massaging the erogenous zones on your partner's body. Do make sure that you are being thorough and are spending some extra time massaging him or her. This will help in building up anticipation and get them excited for more. This will make them come alive with sensations while also experiencing the feeling of being fully grounded. Keep teasing all their senses. The promise that there's more in store will keep them eager about what they can expect and make it interesting.

Make sure that you aren't trying to massage your partner without using massage oil or some form of lubricant because it would be extremely uncomfortable for them and the friction can cause a burning sensation that would not be pleasurable in the slightest. If you are aware that your partner is suffering from some form of a skin condition like a rash or an allergy, then it is best that you avoid massaging them for the time being. It wholly depends on you and your partner the course you would like the massage to take. Keep an open mind while giving or receiving the massage. Don't expect anything, and take things as they come. Only then will you be truly able to experience the real pleasure of a tantric massage.

## Guide to master the techniques

The movements that are made use of in a massage can be

distinguished into two broad categories, and these are old methods and new methods. The general trend is that these two methods are usually combined for developing newer methods. The movements that are used are referred to as manual movements. As is obvious from the name, these movements are performed manually. The main aim of the therapists who have developed these techniques is to please and surprise the recipient, not just with the complexity of the technique that is used but also with its diversity.

The massaging techniques have been accordingly named based on the kind of movement that needs to be made or the tissues that they affect. For instance, there's a massaging technique that is known as softening, and as the name suggests, the movements used in this technique are gentle and soothing. One of the ways in which these techniques are categorized is based on the effects that they tend to have on the body. They are divided into two main groups, and these are Main methods and Secondary techniques.

## Main or fundamental techniques

As the name suggests, these techniques tend to form the base of any massage. These techniques are indispensable for the performance of a massage. The characteristics of the massage might not always be the same, but the techniques used in it are. These particular movements are performed in a methodical manner. It starts off with working on the soft parts, then moves onto the superficial layers, and steadily starts increasing in depth. The five basic techniques that form the base of any massage regardless of the type of massage are mentioned as softening, friction, kneading, battement and vibrations.

## Start with softening

This technique helps in improving the blood flow in the capillaries. Capillaries are small blood vessels that help in transporting blood to all the main organs in the body. This massage helps in improving the flow of blood within these blood vessels. This particular technique requires the massage giver to be very careful and gentle in his movements. The movements should be relaxed and languid. The rhythmic gliding of your hands on the recipient's body will help him relax all the tensed muscles. Apply pressure by making use of your palms or the back of your hands.

## Continuing the rhythm of movements

All massages starts out at a slow pace and softening is a really good technique for getting started. It helps in relaxing the recipient and sets the pace for the rest of the massage. The massaging strokes made use of can be languid, long, leisurely, short, insistent or even vigorous. You shouldn't have to get really worked up about the length of the strokes you are using. A tantric massage is different from a regular massage because of the erotic nature of the massage. So, try and make it different from an ordinary massage. The length and the intensity of the massaging strokes can be slowly altered. Gradually increase their intensity depending upon the state of arousal of the recipient. Tantric massage is all about building anticipation and eagerness in the recipient about what's waiting ahead for them, and this suspense will help in enhancing the pleasure that the recipient experiences.

Generally, the softening technique is made use of during the initial stage of the massage and also at the very end since it has a calming effect. It helps the recipient in relaxing. When you are making use of softening at the end of the massage, simply reverse the movements by starting out with long strokes and moving onto movements that are short and vigorous. This will help the recipient calm down and relax.

Always keep in mind that you should begin and end the massage with the same technique and don't change it. If you have started the massage with softening, then you end it with the same as well. Incorporating this will ensure that the recipient can relax and derive maximum satisfaction from the massage. For making your massage effective, there's one other thing that you can do. The pace at which you are gliding your hands should be at a relatively faster pace than the flow of the blood in the veins. When the blood flow tends to improve, then the recipient will be more relaxed.

The gliding movements used while massaging arms and legs should start from the tips of the fingers and toes and gradually move towards the area where they merge with the torso. While massaging the body, make sure that you follow the veins. It should move downwards, towards the heart. While massaging the neck and throat regions, it should move from the head to shoulders.

## Explanation of the techniques

As mentioned above, the softening technique should be made use of for setting the pace of the massage. This technique can be performed in two different ways. You can perform this either by making use of your fingertips or by making use of your palms and the back of your hands as well.

Either you can hold your fingers closely together, or you can slightly spread them apart as well. This technique is suitable for plain surfaces like the back. You should not exert too much pressure and it should be applied only on the vessels and the nerve endings. If you want to give a deep tissue massage, then make sure that you are using a technique that requires you to exert more pressure like the techniques that are performed with your fists, hands and the outside of your hands as well. Depending upon what the recipient enjoys, you should vary the strokes and the pressure that you are making use of.

## Secondary or completion techniques

The techniques that have been mentioned above are referred to as primary movements. The ones discussed here are referred to as secondary techniques, and they are ancillary to the primary techniques. Both these techniques are equally important. Unless and until they are used in combination with each other, the massage wouldn't be useful. The secondary techniques are ancillary to the fundamental techniques, and their roots are based in the primary techniques. They are mentioned as completion techniques because they help in the completion of the massage that was started by making use of the primary techniques. These are simply the continuation of the previous techniques. Let's take a look at how these techniques should be performed. Some of the most important secondary techniques are sifting and rolling, pressures, shaking, pinching and tractions and tensions.

## Procedure

They can be performed simultaneously or with alternative movements. In the case of alternative movements then, as the name suggests, these movements are performed by alternating between both the hands or by using only one hand at a time and then shifting to the other one. Movements like gliding your hands on the surface can also be done through simultaneous movements or even alternative movements. The movements that are usually made use of throughout the body are referred to as simultaneous movements. This movement involves the use of both the hands at any given point of time and is best suited for massaging the limbs and the back.

Alternative movements can be carried on in three different directions and are classified into long alternative movements, medium alternative movements and short alternative movements. Long alternative movements are the ones that are made in an alternate manner. Only one hand will be made use of for massaging and the other hand stays dormant. This is similar to the simultaneous long movements that are performed at the same time. Medium alternative movements fall somewhere in between the long and short alternative movements. These are longitudinal, slanted and oblique in nature. These movements are best suited for the limbs and the backside. Short alternative movements are short sensual strokes that help you in navigating your partner's body. Like the movements that are made while kissing. These are short alternative movements and are carried out only one at a time. While the rhythm of these slight movement starts to increase the momentum of the languid and long movements decreases. The shorter movements usually exert more pressure than the longer ones. These are made use of for letting the body relax not just from a superficial level but also from the depths. It is usually made use of in treatment of nodes and even in deep tissue massages.

# Chapter 9: Men's Tantric Massage

Tantric massage for men in the initial stage is directed towards helping them open up their chakras and for stimulating their senses. In general, men tend to keep their emotions locked up and instead focus more on their strength and their prowess instead of enjoying the act and they tend to concentrate more on the orgasm instead of enjoying the pleasure they are instrumental in. Also, men tend to hold onto the notion that they are supposed to be active all the time. This makes it really difficult for them to be calm, receptive and not do anything. Tantra teachers tend to give their students different exercises and techniques that can help them in learning to relax, letting go, enjoying the moment and developing a stronger and a deeper bond with their partners. The exercise that's mentioned here is something that all men will enjoy.

Allow for plenty of time for a tantric massage. Set aside a minimum period of two hours, but it is better when there is no time limit as such. Adjust the massage timing in the evening so that neither you nor your partner have got anything else to do and can bask in the afterglow of the massage, or perhaps go to bed while holding each other and fall asleep. Women, this is your chance to not only pleasure your partner but also show them how much you love them and your willingness to pleasure your partner. The objective of this massage isn't about helping your partner reach his orgasm, but it is about providing him with a sensual experience that he will actually enjoy. So, take some time and get everything prepped for this massage.

Before the chosen time of the massage, or when your partner isn't around, you can select a few objects that you can make use of during the massage. You can opt for items that have different textures and are of varying degrees of firmness. A few suggestions would be peacock feathers or any other light feathers, silk scarves, a woolen muffler, marbles, leaves, flowers and so on. Let your imagination run wild. Select items that would feel different against his skin but not uncomfortable or unpleasant.

Just before starting the massage, grab a few scents that you can make him smell, like a fresh orange, cut slices of apple or pear, cinnamon, basil, essential oils or any other scents that you like. Do make sure that the scents that you are opting for are very mild because you are going to be using many scents. Gather six different scents and avoid highly scented items like soaps, concentrated perfumes, incense or even cologne. Don't include a scent that you usually use. The smells should be subtle and natural. Lay them out on a table in the massage room and place a towel over them.

## Lingam massage

A crucial part of the human sexuality is learning about the

penis, loving it and not being afraid of doing so. There are two methods in which the lingam massage can be performed. The first method is for men to learn so that they can practice "peaking" through masturbation. The second method is the one where the partner would give the man a nice relaxing massage. Lingam massage can be thought of like foreplay, or it can also be independent of sex altogether. Most women aren't comfortable with handling a man's penis, and if this is the case, then it would do you some good to set aside a little while to reflect upon the reasons for the negative impressions that you might seem to have about the penis.

Tantra teaches that there needs to be a bond between the partners that is capable of transcending all physical boundaries. It is about connecting with your partner on a personal level and also about connecting with the sexual energy that is present in your partner's body. Lingam massage is one way that will help you in achieving this. Well, to put it simply, lingam massage is a fancy word for referring to a hand job. However, this has to be done with a lot of respect, care, love and yearning for bringing selfless pleasure to your partner. Unlike a regular hand job, Lingam massage includes not just the mere massaging and the stroking of the penis of a man, but it also makes use of and incorporates various other techniques that include the massage of the testicles, the perineum and the prostate.

Lingam is the Sanskrit word that is used for penis, and it means "wand of light" when translated. In the philosophy of Tantra, the penis or the lingam has been approached from a place filled with respect, love and care. The same approach is made use of for a women's yoni or vagina as well. By bringing pleasure to your partner through his lingam, both the partners would be filled with a sexual energy that is a result of the conscious energy between the individuals.

Lingam massage is a particular practice that honors a man, and it is done with the intention of bringing him immense pleasure. There's a lot of sexual energy or chi that is trapped within a man's penis. Learning the ways in which this energy can be stimulated as well as circulated will help in forging a strong bond with your partner.

In fact, in India, there are states of Shiva lingam that are considered to be sacred and are worshiped fervently. The statues of the lingam represent Shiva, one of the most powerful Gods according to Hindu mythology. For most of the people, this lingam also accounts for a pure state of meditation. However, for all the tantric practitioners, this lingam holds a secret meaning. It depicts all the energy that is trapped in a man's body and is considered to contain masculine essence, and it is all concentrated in one place.

Therefore, if you want sex to become a sacred experience, then you will need to adopt an approach towards a man's penis that would treat his body as a temple wherein the all powerful sexual energy of the cosmos rests. Lingam massage isn't about having an orgasm or about performing a sexual act. Instead, it is all about trying to find more pleasure and it is about feeling more in general, that will in turn become a wave of immense pleasure. Here are the steps that can be followed for giving a lingam massage.

The first method is for men who would want to make use of this sacred method for cultivating and harnessing the divine energy through masturbation. The same approach can also be made use of by the giver of the massage as well.

### *Relaxing*

The first step is to get your partner to lie on his back on a stable surface. It could be the bed or even a massaging table. Prop a pillow under his head and a pillow can also be propped under his hips. He needs to lie down in such a manner that his legs are slightly spread apart, and his knees are bent so that it gives the massage giver an unobstructed and unrestricted view of the male genitalia. Keep reminding your partner to breathe deeply because this will help in relaxing further.

### *Breathe deeply*

Breathing is one aspect that distinguishes the practice of Tantra from regular sex. While the giver is trying to perform a lingam massage, it is really important that the receiver is breathing deeply. For increasing his pleasure, as well as his state of arousal, it is crucial that both the partners are breathing deeply and slowly. When the giver inhales, she will be receiving all of his sexual energy and arousals and loving energy is transferred to him when she exhales. This simple breathing technique has three benefits. It will help in reaching a deeper level of meditation and mindfulness. It will make the giver more empathetic towards the thoughts and feelings of the receiver. Lastly, it will help in improving the sexual intuition of the massage giver and make her more aware of what her partner wants.

### *Your partner should breathe deeply*

Before starting the lingam massage, the giver has to tune into her partner by following the breathing technique that was explained in the previous step. Just by taking a few deep breaths in a synchronized manner this will help in putting you both at ease and will help you relax. While the giver is performing the massage, she can keep constantly reminding him to relax fully.

### *Lubricating his penis*

You can make use of your favorite massaging oil. Refer to the earlier chapters for helping you choose the perfect massaging oil. Make use of this oil for lubricating his shaft and his testicles as well. Start the massage by simply sliding your hands up and then down his thighs before moving onto the good stuff. This will make your partner relax, and you can also keep complimenting him about you are seeing and what you appreciate. After massaging his thighs for a few minutes, move onto his testicles and massage them gently. You can make use of your fingernails for slightly grazing his sack or your fingers for slightly tugging them. Alternatively, you can cup these in your hands and fondle them gently. You can massage the area around and between the testicles. This is the perineum, the area that lies between the testicles and the anus. While handling his testicles, be careful. Men tend to react differently, and some might be more sensitive or even ticklish than others. So, ask him about how he likes it while massaging or fondling his testicles.

### *Massaging the shaft*

Once you have gently massaged the area around the receiver's penis and you can see that he wants more, that's when you have to shift your attention towards the shaft of his penis. Change your grip from hard to light and vice versa. Keep varying the sequence in which you are stroking him from up and down, and then a twisting motion. Shift your hands and when you are using one hand, vary the speed. Shift from left to right and then from right to left hand. Keep varying the speed of the strokes from slow to fast. Initially, you can make use of slow strokes for building up the rhythm and then move quickly. Keep alternating the speed, rhythm; the pressure applied, and the technique used. Shift the shaft strokes as well. You can start from the root either to the top or from the head to the base. Once you have reached the head of the penis, move your hand towards the base and while reaching the base make a twisting motion. Variety is the key, so keep making variations.

When you are making use of two hands, then you can massage his shaft in a few different ways. Both hands can hold the penis in the same direction, and the fingers should be pointing in the same direction. One hand can hold the penis facing in one direction, and the other can hold the penis facing the other way. Both the hands can move in an up and down motion. Make use of massage oil to lubricate his penis well. One hand can move from the head to the base while the other hand is making a twisting motion at the very tip of the penis.

### *Keep him on edge*

You would have noticed that by now he would be worked up and might be eager for the sweet release. If you have been paying close attention to the way his body moves, his breathing and the sounds he is making, you will be able to predict whether or not he's nearing his climax. When you notice that he is at the very edge, that's when you will need to slow down or stop what you are doing and gently remind him to keep breathing deeply and let him ride the wave of pleasurable feelings that he might be experiencing. His penis might go from being fully erect to being semi-hard. Don't worry; this is natural.

### *Start stimulating his Sacred Spot*

The prostate is a man's Sacred Spot. This is a small gland that is located between the bladder and his penis. When this walnut-sized gland is stimulated properly, it is quite pleasurable. Internal access can also be gained to the prostate, and it can be done by inserting a finger into his anus or even with the help of a sex toy that's used for massaging the prostate. You will find more information about prostate massage in the next chapter. If your partner isn't familiar with a prostate massage, then start externally. You can find the sacred spot by looking for a slight indentation that would be present somewhere between the testicles and the anus. It would be about the size of a pea or a walnut. Gently push this inward and go slow while doing this. Once you have successfully found the spot, you can start massaging it slowly with your fingers and knuckles. Make use of a circular motion and use a lot of massaging oil while doing so. If you can get your partner to shave, it would be relatively easy to find this spot.

### *Stimulating the prostate internally*

If your partner is willing or is curious to try a prostate massage, then you can turn up the heat with a prostate massage. If he is up for it, then you will want to start out by loosening up his anus to allow entry to your fingers. Start out by gently massaging the outside of his anus in a circular motion. Insert a finger slowly only if he is ready for it. Do make sure that his anus is well oiled before you try inserting your finger. Also, make sure that your nails aren't sharp or long as this might hurt him. Start out with just the tip of one finger if he seems to be enjoying it and then move it along slowly. The prostate is about two or three inches inside the anus, so you will need to probe a little deeper. Start caressing the prostate by moving your finger(s) in a come hither motion. Prostate massage will be pleasurable for your partner, but he needs to be willing to go along with it. Read the next chapter to understand more about it.

### *End the massage*

For ending the massaging, you can let your partner ejaculate, or you can also transition onto sex. It all depends on what you and your partner feel like doing at that given point of time.

## Prostate Massage

Tantric massage is a holistic massage that helps in transmitting the raw sexual energy that's present in the body into energies that are more subtle. Conscious breathing enables in the happening of this transformation. Erotic energy is usually associated with moving towards the goal of achieving an orgasm. This particular goal orientation tends to create unnecessary tensions as well as tightness in the body that tends to block out the natural flow of energy in the body and restricts the movement of the sexual energy as well. Tantric practices will help a person in letting go of this goal orientation and allow for a condition that provides for surrender of control to the natural flow of energy in the body. The key to doing it is to be present in the moment when there's a buildup of arousal while also helping in directing this flow of energy. It takes a lot of time and energy as well as commitment and practice to change this condition.

Tantric massage makes use of sensual touch that's combined with conscious breathing. This is a potent combination that activates all the neuromuscular pathways in the body and reinforces these connections each time a pleasurable activity has been experienced. This is the reason for the expansion of our ability to receive pleasure throughout our life. However, the genital areas are usually desensitized, and this prevents achieving higher pleasure. This particular desensitization is known as genital armoring.

Due to circumcision, feelings of fear or guilt associated with masturbation, inept prostatic examinations and even the compulsion to demonstrate their masculinity tends to result in genital armoring in men. This condition can manifest itself in different ways; it could lead to the hardening of the penis, penis insensitivity, oversensitivity, fragility of the foreskin or even erectile dysfunction. It could also manifest itself in the form of chronic tension in the muscles in their anal sphincter. This condition doesn't do any good, and it stems from unnecessary expectations that are thrust upon men by the society that we live in. Men tend to have a lot of armoring even in their heart area, and this means that they will be unable to experience any pleasurable sensations that are generated in their genital regions. They will never be able to experience pleasure truly and fully.

Once the penis has been fully healed, it becomes flexible, warm and vibrant as it is supposed to be. It becomes alive when it is erect. In addition to all the stimulation that is provided during sexual intercourse and activity, increased sensitivity also helps a man to experience pleasure like never before and he gets to receive pleasure by simply resting his penis in the vagina in a non-demanding and a relaxed way. Before healing, he might not have been able to feel much of this pleasure or even maintain his arousal for long. In both men as well as women, only when their genitals are healed and when there's no pressure of performance, will they be able to truly enjoy the experience.

Until the whole genital, as well as anal regions, have been cleared of all the negative imprints left behind by negative experiences, it would be impossible for a person to enjoy the erotic experience. Love and acceptance are key to sexual healing. When this is combined with a direct and a hands-on massage, it leads to healing all the old wounds and allows the individual to experience ecstasy.

Tantric massage helps in breaking down the barriers of genital armoring that lead to sexual dysfunctions. If any unnecessary emotions are trapped in these areas, even this can cause genital armoring. For instance, feelings of anger and even rejection from broken relationships in the past can be held in the genital region and this can hold a person back from experiencing the sexual act or even give themselves to their partner fully.

## Prostate Massage Ritual

The main purpose of this massage is to awaken all the dormant sexual potential that is held within the prostate gland. The prostate gland can be considered as the doorway towards unlocking a man's true sexual potential. The prostate is also referred to as the sacred spot and can be compared to the female G-Spot. Unfortunately, most heterosexual men tend to consider this body part to be off limits completely. This attitude is often the result of a homophobic culture that propagates that if a man derives pleasure through his anal area, it means that he is gay. This taboo that is associated with this erogenous zone instills fear in the minds of men. Anal and Prostate Massage can help a man release all the dormant sexual energy that must be stored within them and once this barrier is removed only then will he be able to enjoy sex as it is supposed to be. There are many benefits of prostate and anal massage. It can help in dealing with issues like erectile dysfunction, imbalances caused due to stress, ejaculation control, lack of any sexual desire, inability to receive pleasure, difficulty in being intimate, emotional blocks, mood swings and so on. All the negative feelings related to being sexual can be relieved through this form of massage. Let us learn more about this massage.

The G-Spot of a man is the prostate gland, and according to the tantric philosophy, it is his center of sexual emotions. Massaging a man's prostate can help in releasing a lot of pent-up emotional as well as physical stress. When this is coupled with the additional stimulation that he would receive through his penis, and then massage his prostate; it would be pleasurable for him. The only direct way in which you can stimulate or massage a man's sacred spot is by going through his anus. This definitely will take time for getting acclimatized to being penetrated through the anus. This might not be for every man. The benefits of a prostate massage are numerous and it can be a pleasurable and a sensual experience. For lovers or even tantric partners, massaging of this particular sacred spot can be quite a powerful experience. It is not only pleasurable for the receiver but is quite empowering for the giver as well.

The prostate is the walnut-sized gland that is located right under the bladder, and it isn't far away from the internal root of the penis as well. The gland is close to the rectal wall and therefore reaching it through the anus is easy. The reasons are as follows.

Regardless of the method that you would make use of for touching the prostate, the closest indirect access is through the rectal wall, and this means that there would still be a membrane that would be in the way. Despite this particular restriction, the prostate is sensitive to any form of pressure. This means that it can be stimulated by pressing, touching, probing, or even by simply stroking the gland through the rectal wall. It helps in producing sublime feelings that a man would experience during ejaculation. Along with the genital areas, even the anus has an intricate network of millions of nerve endings in the body that can yield a lot of pleasure. Many don't know this, but about one-third of the penis is hidden inside the body, and the base of this hidden penis can be stimulated in the same manner as the prostate. The effect of stimulating the prostate, penis, and the hidden penis would have a brilliant effect on the man. There are certain psychological feelings that a man needs to get used to for enjoying a prostate massage. It also acts as a mental stimulant and this rush is caused because of the notion that the man is placing himself in an extremely vulnerable position that can be quite exciting for both the receiver and the massage giver as well. Men are naturally more dominating and controlling, and being placed in such a submissive and vulnerable position is unaccustomed for them and would be cherished by the giver of the massage.

## *Preparation*

This is an intimate ritual and certain rules would apply to it as well. The receiver of the massage should be clean and the giver should have surgical gloves on, the tight fitting sort. It is crucial that the giver wears gloves to protect the receiver's delicate membrane from their fingernails and also the rough skin as well. If the surface is well lubricated, then it allows for easier motion. The receiver should take a shower before the massage, and this will also help in building up anticipation for what is yet to come.

## *Positions*

Face to face: For greater intimacy, you should opt for this position. Once you have fully undressed, the receiver should be seated, and his back needs to be reclined and should be supported by pillows placed at a 45-degree angle. Ask him to pull his knees towards his chest, and they should be slightly angled out. The resulting position needs to be comfortable for both the parties involved. The giver should also have an unrestricted view and access to the anus as well as the receiver's genitals. The giver can either sit cross-legged or even kneel in front of the receiver. For relaxing the receiver, the giver can start out by slowly massaging the lower parts of the receiver's body, especially the area around their abdomen. During the initial phase, the receiver can opt to close his eyes, but later on, it is crucial for the receiver and the giver to maintain eye contact. The giver gets to decide when the receiver has been fully aroused and relaxed as well. Once the receiver is aroused, the giver should put on the gloves and then start lubricating the anus of the receiver. The process of lubrication shouldn't be rushed and it should be done slowly. Start out with a circular motion and start stroking the anal entrance gently. The primary objective of this motion is to get the rosebud to relax. The giver shouldn't ever poke at the anus using the fingertip. However, she should keep on applying constant pressure with the pad of the finger. Constant lubrication and steady pressure will allow the anus to relax and then the finger can easily enter. It does take a while, so be patient. When it is time, the giver will observe that the finger seems to easily enter the anal canal without any obstruction from the anal sphincter. The giver shouldn't try to move the finger in and out of the anus and should instead keep it still. The giver should remove the finger only for the purpose of adding more lubrication.

The next step is for the giver to seek out the prostate of the receiver. This can be done easily by slightly crooking the finger that is inserted and feeling for a roundish and a rectangular protrusion that is an inch or two inside the rectum. Keep applying pressure to the prostate and it will generate different sensations that would push the receiver closer to an impending orgasm. The giver will be able to control these sensations by varying the pressure that is being applied to the prostate. The ability to control the receiver's ejaculation is through the manipulation of the prostate. The giver can massage the receiver's penis or the receiver can do that on his own. During this cycle of arousal, the giver can start to move the finger slowly in and out of the anus to stimulate more feelings and this will stimulate the nerve endings that are in and around the anus. It is critical that at this stage in the massage, eye contact needs to be made. Three scenarios can play out. The first one would be where the giver allows the receiver to masturbate for achieving an orgasm. The giver can provide verbal encouragement. The second scenario is one where the giver can masturbate the receiver's penis with one hand while stimulating his anus with the other. The third one is where the receiver might want to his penis to be stimulated but not directly. Gently stroking each lobe will help in stimulating the flow of semen through the erect penis.

Facing away: This is a position where the receiver has got to kneel, with his knees apart and butt elevated, while his elbows are resting on a flat surface, like a soft floor mat with cushioning. This position should be comfortable for both the parties involved in the massage. The giver might decide to kneel or even sit in a spread-eagled manner and should be positioned behind the receiver. This would allow the giver to have unrestricted access to the receiver's anus. The giver should also be able to reach between the receiver's legs and stimulate his genitals as well. From then on, it's the same as the previous method.

# Chapter 10: Women's Tantric Massage

## Yoni Massage

Yoni is the Sanskrit word that's used for vagina, and it translates into "sacred temple" or sacred space. Tantra teachings view yoni from a perspective of immense respected and love. Men, in particular, should learn about this. Before getting started with a yoni massage, it is really important to create an environment and space that would help the receiver, in this case, the woman, relax. She won't be able to reach a heightened state of sexual arousal and experience pleasure unless and until she is truly relaxed.

The giver will also experience the joy of giving his partner immense pleasure and also gets to witness it. The yoni massage is also used as a means of developing a bond that depends on trust and intimacy. It has also been used by massage therapists and, as well as sex therapists, as a means through which they can assist women who have endured sexual trauma or suffer from any sexual blocks. The aim of a yoni massage isn't just to achieve an orgasm. In fact, an orgasm just happens to be an excellent and welcome side effect of yoni massage. The giver and the receiver of the massage can relax and neither of them has got to worry about achieving an orgasm. For this reason, the orgasm tends to be powerful and intense when it ultimately occurs. If the giver also doesn't expect anything in return, the receiver can fully enjoy the massage.

### *The Massage*

The receiver has got to lie on her back, and her head can be propped up with the help of pillows so that she has got a view of her genitals and her partner as well. Take a pillow and cover it with a towel, then place this pillow under her hips. Her legs need to be slightly spread apart so that her knees are slightly bent and genitals should be exposed. This position would give the giver an unrestricted access to his lover's Yoni and other parts of her body as well. Taking deep breaths will help in calming the giver as well as the receiver. Do remember to keep breathing deeply to make sure that you and your partner are both relaxed throughout this process. The giver will then have to gently remind the receiver to start breathing slowly and deeply and if the receiver starts taking shallow breaths, he can gently remind her again. Deep breathing will help in staying calm and it will also prevent hyperventilation.

Start by gently massaging your partner's legs, thighs, abdomen, breasts and other erogenous zones. Encourage her to relax, and this will allow you to to prepare for the massage. Take the massage oil or the lubricant of your choice in your hand and then pour it over her yoni. Pour a little oil so that it drips down over the outer lips of her vagina and covers it. Start by gently massaging her mound and the outer lips as well. Don't rush your moves and take some time. You will need to let her relax and give into the massage. Squeeze the outer lip between your thumb and index finger, but do so gently. Then you will have to glide your finger up the length of her yoni. Repeat the same to the inner lips of her vagina. Don't be in a hurry and take your time doing this. It would be helpful if the receiver and the giver can maintain eye contact during the massage for as long as possible. The receiver should give her input regarding the pressure, the strokes, speed, depth, etc. or the need to be decreased or increased. Don't engage in any casual conversations and make sure that you are limiting this and should instead concentrate on the buildup of pleasurable sensations; too much talking might kill the mood.

The clitoris is the crown jewel, and it shouldn't be neglected. The clitoris is similar to the male glans, but it is four times more sensitive than the glans. It has around 6000 to 8000 nerve endings, so it obviously is extremely sensitive. This hypersensitive nodule has got only one purpose, and it is pleasure. It can receive and transmit pleasure like no other part of the body. Start stroking the clit in a clockwise direction with circles and then do the same in a counterclockwise motion. Gently squeeze this little nub between your index finger and your thumb. This is a part of the massage and it isn't done with the intention of getting the receiver off. Well, the receiver will undoubtedly be incredibly aroused by this action, but keep encouraging her to relax and take deep breaths.

Slowly and gently, the giver has got to insert his middle finger of his right hand into the vagina. There's a reason why the right hand has got to be used. It is associated with polarity in Tantra. Start gently exploring and massaging the insides of her vagina. Take your time and be gentle with your movements. Vary the pressure, speed, depth and the direction. This massage helps in nurturing as well as relaxing her yoni. The middle finger of the giver would be inserted in the receiver's yoni, with the palm facing upwards, the giver has got to crook his middle finger in a "come here" gesture and keep massaging her yoni. The giver's finger would come in contact with the spongy tissue that is present in the pubic bone, just behind the clit. This is referred to as the G-spot or the Sacred Spot. She will experience immense pleasure if this particular spot is massaged properly. Vary the pressure and the pattern of movement to elicit a different reaction from her. After a while, the giver can also insert another finger. Most women wouldn't have any problem with two fingers being inserted into their yoni because it merely provides them more stimulation. For additional stimulation, the giver can gently insert a finger into her anus and rub her anus with his right pinky finger. If you feel that your partner might have any objections about this, then don't do this without her prior consent.

Make use of your left hand for massaging her breasts, abdomen and clitoris. If you are massaging her clitoris, then it is best advised that you make use of your thumb and move it around in an up and down motion, while the rest of your hand is lying on her mound. The dual stimulation that is provided by both your hands will provide incredible pleasure to the receiver. Keep on massaging, and you can vary the speed and pressure of the strokes. Don't forget to maintain eye contact through this all. Make sure that you are breathing deeply and be gentle with her. Some women tend to have had negative sexual experiences, and they need to be healed. A gentle and loving massage is the best way in which you can make her feel loved and cherished. Continue with the massage even if she has an orgasm and don't stop. Multiple orgasms might also occur depending upon the intensity of the massage. Towards the end, start massaging her slowly and gently. Let your lover relax and bask in the afterglow of the Yoni massage. Cuddling or even holding her body will help in soothing her. As you learn to master this particular technique of massaging, it will help in enriching your sex life.

## Tantric Breast Massage

The Tantric breast massage is a ritual that would allow a woman to receive sensual energy as well as unconditional love from her partner. The breast massage is a special type of tantric massage that focuses on the woman's bosom. Massaging the breasts not only makes them firmer, but it also improves their health and helps in maintaining the much-needed balance of hormones in a woman's body. Breast massage can also be thought of as a great way in which a man can pleasure, heal and also form an intimate bond with his partner. The breasts can be thought of as the seat of a woman's sexuality and they need to be loved and honored before any other part of her body could be opened up to her partner.

The breast massage can be slightly tricky because the breast tissues are delicate. However, if this has been done properly, and by exerting a moderate amount of pressure, then it would be quite pleasurable and simple as well. The space that you have chosen for doing the breast massage should be warm, inviting and intimate. It should be a place where your partner feels welcome and comfortable as well. Before you start the massage, express to your partner that the massage is purely for her pleasure, that she should enjoy it, and shouldn't think about anything else.

Start the massage by gently resting one of your hands on the woman's heart and the other on her yoni and visualize the energy moving from your heart to your hand, and finally to her heart and her yoni. This visualization helps in connecting to your partner and has a healing effect and always makes use of it at the very beginning of the breast massage. For avoiding friction and any form of discomfort, make use of massage oil on the skin. Gently apply the massage oil onto her skin, and this is the first stage of the massage. The oil needs to be applied in circular motions; the direction of the motion should be from the center of the breast to the region towards the underarms. Keep caressing your partner's breasts slowly and gently, while brushing your palms over the whole of her breast for creating a wonderful sensation. Establish a rhythm and keep repeating the moves consistently. If you are working in a clockwise motion, then maintain the same motion on both the breasts. There is another move that you can try, you will need to place your palm over her entire breast such that the nipple happens to be in the center of your palm and then fan out your fingers as if they are the spokes of a wheel. Now, gently bring them towards the center and finish it off with a gentle tug at the end. Repeat this.

The second step would be to start massaging the breast once it has been fully covered in massage oil. The breast then needs to be kneaded in a gentle manner by lifting it slightly off the chest and then pressing it down delicately with both your hands. The other variation that you can try is holding the breasts in both your hands, and then gently twisting and kneading the breasts.

The third step is to try and massage the flesh as if you are scooping out the breast by making use of your fingertips. The strokes should be really gentle and not rough. The strokes should be done in clockwise motion and then in anti-clockwise motion.

The fourth step of the massage would be to start massaging the nipples. Your thumbs should be placed on opposite sides of your partner's nipples. Start by gently massaging the outside, around her areola. Slowly and gently, move your thumbs closer and gently squeeze her nipple between your thumbs and tug it towards yourself. Keep repeating this until you have managed to make a full circle around her nipples. Depending upon the way your partner reacts, you will have to manage the pressure that you are using.

The skin around the breasts should be stroked and smoothed out, by making use of your fingertips you should move them towards the center of the breast and then away from it. Repeat the same steps with the other breast as well.

You should end the breast massage in the same manner in which you had begun. End it by placing your hands on her heart and the other on her yoni. Visualize the warm energy from your heart move to your hand and from there to her heart and yoni. Keep breathing slowly and deeply and allow her to rest for a while after this. Breast massage is an enjoyable experience for both the giver and the receiver. It has a healing nature on both a mental and physical level. It is also a wonderful form of relaxation for your partner and is very easy to perform. Combine this with any other form of erotic massage if you feel like.

# Chapter 11: Improving Your Sex Life

Do you feel that your sex life feels superficial? Do you feel that there's no real connection between you and your partner when you are having sex? Do you not feel any love while engaging in lovemaking? Do you feel that lovemaking should be more than a physical act and it should help you in discovering more about yourself? Are you afraid of opening up your sexuality fully? Would you like sex to be more about finding soulful bliss and not just physical pleasure? Do you want to enjoy the real beauty and grace of lovemaking? Do you feel that your relationship has become more meaningful but your lovemaking hasn't? If your answer is yes to these questions, then the wisdom you seek can only be found in tantric. The conventional sex advice can't help you remedy the above problems. A tantric massage will help you learn about your sexual state.

A tantric massage will help your body become more sensitive, and will intensify the feelings. You will be able to develop your body for experiencing varying levels of sexual sensations, enjoying a more fulfilling and enriching sexual experience, feeling a deeper connection with your partner while having sex, connecting your body and soul through sex and becoming more open while having sex. It will help in perceiving a physical love while engaged in the physical act of sex, expressing a nurturing love during this process, getting rid of all emotional and mental barriers that didn't allow you to enjoy. You will give yourself up entirely to the act of lovemaking, discovering a new dimension of sensitivity and sensuality that is quite nourishing and having a whole body sexual experience.

Making use of the tantric massage can help you in improving your love life. This erotic massage technique has been in use for centuries and was developed in ancient India thousands of years ago. This practice has once again gained popularity and is an age-old technique used for bringing pleasure. Tantric massage is a technique that is followed by all practitioners of tantric teachings all over the world. This erotic massage is helpful in building up your awareness about your sexuality and also in helping you to reach a state of absolute sexual bliss. The massage simply focuses on the erogenous zones of your body along with all the other parts, and this will truly make you feel more relaxed and put you in a state of arousal.

Incorporate tantric massage into your regular sex life. Tantric massage provides the much-required sexual build up for engaging in sexual intercourse. Sex is so much more than the physical act of joining of the bodies; Tantra believes that it is the union of two people on a physical, emotional, mental, and a spiritual level. Tantric massage will help you in doing so. All the problems that you might have been facing in the sexual department can be remedied with the help of this ancient art form.

# Chapter 12: Aromatherapy Massage

Aromatherapy makes use of various essential oils that are believed to have certain healing properties. Concentrated essences of various flower, fruits, leaves, seeds and even barks are made use of for making these aromatic oils. There are about 400 different essential oils, but only about 40 are made use of in aromatherapy. Practitioners of aromatherapy firmly believe that an aromatherapy massage will help in getting rid of all the accumulated stress, boost a person's well-being and it also helps in rejuvenating the body. The different essentials oils that are derived from plants are made use of in aromatherapy for harnessing the therapeutic benefits that they offer. In an aromatherapy massage, the essential oils are usually mixed with a carrier oils like sweet almond oil, coconut oil, or even grapeseed oil. For a relaxing session of aromatherapy, two of the popular choices of essential oils are lavender and bergamot. Peppermint and eucalyptus oils can be made use of for a massage for helping with sore muscles. The oils that are to be made use of would purely depend upon the desired outcome of the massage or even based upon the particular problem it is supposed to help with. Learning about a person's current state of physical and mental health, their daily routine will help in selecting the perfect massage oil. Take into consideration the different properties of the essential oils before making use of one. Information about all this has been given in the previous chapters. Therefore, you can make use of that information for selecting massage oils.

There are a couple of different theories that try to explain how an aromatherapy massage would work. The first theory states that the essential oils are directly absorbed into your body through your skin and then into the bloodstream. Once they are in the blood stream, then they travel throughout your body and have a specific effect on a particular body part or organ.

Aromatherapy massage is a form of an alternative therapeutic practice that makes use of different natural properties to the essential oils. Aromatherapy combines these beneficial therapeutic properties of essential oils with the healing benefits of a massage. The massage receiver is usually nude during this massage, and it only has a strong physical effect on the body, but it also has positive emotional and mental effects as well. It is often described to be extremely relaxing. There are different health benefits of an aromatherapy massage. It helps in dealing with several nervous and circulatory conditions, along with lymphatic, immune, circulatory, as well as muscular systems present in the body. Aromatherapy, when done well, will make the recipient feel relaxed, obtain some mental clarity, alleviate bad headaches, and get rid of all the unnecessary stress that we all tend to carry within ourselves.

Certain basic massage therapy steps should be followed for getting the best benefits. A full body aromatherapy massage session can take anywhere between one to one and a half hours. The techniques made use of in an aromatherapy massage would depend upon the requirements of the recipient. The massage should always be adapted according to the different needs of the recipient. Here are a few basic steps that you should follow during the massage.

## Basic steps before aromatherapy massage

It is crucial that the massage giver understands the reason for the massage. There might be a specific reason for getting the massage. If the massage receiver were getting an aromatherapy massage for its various therapeutic benefits, then it would be helpful to understand if the receiver has any health problems. If the receiver is getting it in order to improve the intimacy quotient or for simply relaxing, then the massaging technique made use of should be such that it addresses the desired issues. The oil that you are making use of would also depend upon the specific requirements of the massage receiver. Selecting the right oil is crucial for an effective massage. Make sure that all the necessary items and things that you will need during the massage are handy. Keep a few hand towels, napkins and tissues nearby. Play some soothing background music that will create a more relaxed atmosphere. The atmosphere should be conducive of the massage and should let the individual relax. The next step would be to opt for the perfect technique for the massage. The techniques used will depend upon the experience of the giver and also the requirements of the receiver. Before starting the massage take some time and both the giver and receiver should take about each other's expectations from the massage. It is really important that the massage receiver is relaxed and comfortable throughout the massage. Since the receiver would be nude for the duration, make sure that the room temperature isn't cold but warm and pleasant.

## Steps for giving a full body massage

Here are a few aromatherapy massage steps that can be made use of during a full body massage.

The first step would be having a long talk with the massage receiver regarding their expectations from the massage and any problem that they would like to address. The massage receiver needs to be comfortable and should be comfortably lying on a massage table with a sheet or a towel spread over them. Alternatively, they can remain nude as well. The session would start with an effleurage massage beginning from the ankles and moving towards the hips and upwards. Make use of slow and strong strokes for massaging limbs. Then move over to the spine and start massaging gently. Make use of fingers, knuckles, palms, and the backs of hands for working out the tissues for relieving hidden tension. The next step would be to start massaging the hands and arms of the receiver. Make use of techniques like effleurage, compression, friction and petrissage. After this, the receiver would have to assume a face-up position. The receiver's neck, shoulders, and head should be massaged carefully. Avoid sensitive areas like the throat. Move on to massaging the jaw line, ears, area behind the ears, bridge of the nose and the brows along with temples should be gently massaged. Usually, this massage is ended with a foot massage. Once you are done giving the massage, you will need to simply rinse off the oil from your hands.

## Tips to be observed after the session is over

Regardless of whether or not it was a full body massage or a partial body massage, certain after-care tips should be observed.

Avoid having a bath for the next eight hours after the massage. The essential oils made use of usually take a while to penetrate the dermis and for entering the bloodstream. A bath will help in washing off the residual oils that might be left on the skin. Aromatherapy helps in detoxifying the body, therefore for deriving the best benefits, make sure that you haven't consumed any alcohol or smoked any cigarettes. Give your body a chance to cleanse itself. If any phototoxic oils have been used in the massage, then do not expose your skin to any sunlight or any harsh lights. For deepening the cleansing benefits that aromatherapy offers, make sure that you are drinking plenty of herbal teas and water. Water is the best way for detoxifying your body. Avoid having rich and heavy foods. Let your body eliminate toxic substances and consume fresh fruits and vegetables that will help with this process. A session of aromatherapy massage will leave you feeling relaxed and tired, in a good way. Getting some rest after the massage will help in revitalizing your body. Give your body a break once in a while for relaxing and rejuvenating itself.

## Precautions to be taken

Certain precautions should be taken while giving or performing an aromatherapy massage. Here are a few safety precautions that will help you in giving the massage receiver all the benefits that an aromatherapy massage has got to offer. For doing this, the first thing that you can do is test a small patch of the receiver's skin for ascertaining any allergies that the individual might have. Also, check for any cuts or any other wounds that might be there. It is best to avoid such areas while giving the massage. If the receiver happens to be pregnant or suffers from any other severe health problem, then it is better to consult their doctor before giving this massage. It is helpful if you can set some ground rules regarding any boundaries that should be maintained during the duration of the massage. For avoiding any uncomfortable experiences, it is advisable that the massage giver and receiver should sit down and discuss the massage, the things that the giver should and should not do. Before giving a massage, make sure that the sheets are clean, the towels used are fresh and the equipment made use of is clean.

An aromatherapy massage is effective. This massage helps in stimulating all the sensory organs and helps the body and mind to relax. Different people tend to have different psychological effects and responses to a session of aromatherapy massage. Aromatherapy massage is incredibly relaxing, soothing, calming, and an overall enjoyable experience. This particular massage makes use of all our sensory organs to create a positive effect on an individual on physical and a metal level as well. The different steps of an aromatherapy massage would not be effective if the proper essential oils aren't used. The effectiveness of the massage equally depends upon the techniques and also the oils used. If you want this massage to have a positive impact, then you will need to let go of yourself and indulge your senses in this full-body massage. Just like with any other tantric practice, aromatherapy massage would not be effective if you don't give yourself the permission to let go of all your worries and stress. Let go and enjoy this massage.

# Conclusion

I would like to thank you once again for purchasing this book!

The core philosophy of Tantra is not just about seeking pleasure, but it is also a form of love as well as worship. Worship in this context has no religious reference; it simply means showering your partner with attention and paying homage to your partner's body. The sexual high that you will receive will be like nothing that you have ever experienced. Your time will be spent well indeed. Tantra is so much more than the general notion that people possess. It is not about sex and it also includes the practice of tantric massage.

By now, you would have understood the concept of tantric massage. Tantric massage will help you connect with your partner and also the Cosmos. All your senses will be filled with different sensations and feelings that you have never experienced. There is nothing better than feeling the pleasure that your partner is experiencing and lying beside your partner as he/she is basking in the afterglow. The knowledge that you have given them such pleasure will do some good to your ego and will make you feel good about yourself. Tantra will help you understand that the best thing that you can give your partner is your true self, without any façade or pretenses. This is the greatest gift that you can give your partner. Yourself, your body, mind and soul without holding anything back. This feeling of being in sync with your partner on an emotional and spiritual level will work wonders for your relationship. Tantra transcends physical boundaries of the mortal realm.

Tantra is about so much more than the physical attributes.

Tantric massage will help in bringing you closer to your lover in ways you never thought of before. This will have a positive impact on all the aspects of your relationship including your sex life. Your sex life will no longer be monotonous, it will be exciting, and you will be able to discover the true meaning of being in sync with your partner. Tantric massage is one simple way in which you can incorporate Tantra into your life. Tantric massage is about pushing the physical boundaries of pleasure without actually engaging in sexual intercourse. It will help you in prolonging your shared pleasure and help you in connecting with your partner on a spiritual level. A bond like this cannot be broken.

Tantric massage is a relatively simple concept once you have understood the basics and with a little bit of practice, you will be able to experience pleasure like never before. Make sure that you and your partner have discussed it before getting started. It is quite important to make sure that you are both comfortable with it and remember to keep communicating openly about what you feel if you really want this technique to work out.

I hope that this book has provided you all the information about tantric massage and the manner in which it can be made use of for doubling your pleasure. All that is left for you to do is give it a try.

Thank you and all the best!

52193222R00060

Made in the USA
San Bernardino, CA
13 August 2017